Missy Hyatt
First Lady of Wrestling

Missy Hyatt
with Charles Salzberg and Mark Goldblatt

ECW Press

Copyright © Missy Hyatt, 2001

All rights reserved. No part of this publication may be reproduced, stored in a retrieval system, or transmitted in any form by any process — electronic, mechanical, photocopying, recording, or otherwise — without the prior written permission of the copyright owners and ECW Press.

NATIONAL LIBRARY OF CANADA CATALOGUING IN PUBLICATION DATA

Hyatt, Missy
Missy Hyatt : first lady of wrestling

ISBN 1-55022-498-0

1. Hyatt, Missy 2. Wrestlers – United States. 3. Wrestling – United States – Biography. I. Title.

GV1196.H92A3 2001   796.812'092   C2001-902844-X

Layout by Mary Bowness

Printed by Printcrafters, Winnipeg

Distributed in Canada by
General Distribution Services,
325 Humber College Blvd.,
Toronto, ON M9W 7C3

Distributed in the United States by
LPC Group
1436 West Randolph Street,
Chicago, IL USA 60607

Published by ECW Press
2120 Queen Street East, Suite 200
Toronto, ON M4E 1E2
ecwpress.com

This book is set in Futura and Imago.

PRINTED AND BOUND IN CANADA

The publication of *Missy Hyatt* has been generously supported by the Government of Canada through the Book Publishing Industry Development Program. Canada

Contents

1 Sweet Melissa
Florida and Georgia, unaffiliated   1

2 Learning the Ropes
Dallas, WCCW   21

3 Living on Tulsa Time
Oklahoma, UWF   41

4 Wrestling with the Mania
New York, WWF   57

5 Ain't No Place I'd Rather Be
Oklahoma and Tennessee, UWF/NWA and USWA   77

6 Alabama Getaway
Alabama, CWF   91

7 Ted and Missy's Bogus Journey
Georgia, WCW   103

8 Taken to the Extreme
New York and Pennsylvania, ECW   141

9 Indie-Cent Exposure
Northeast, Independent Organizations   157

Acknowledgments

All right, this is the cheesy part where I thank people who have made a difference in my life. So first of all, I'd like to thank my family — without their love, support and encouragement I would have never pursued my dreams. Thanks to my mother and father, my sister Vonda, her husband Lyle, and her sons Nicholas and Lee, and his wife June. Also, the Geiser gang: Michelle, Tracy, Michael, Andrea and Ed.

I'd also like to thank my writers Mark and Charles; without them, I would never have been able to put my thoughts to paper. (Reading the first draft scared me because it was just like talking to myself!) Thanks, too, to my agents Peter Rubie and June Clark, Joe Gannon for his disk work, and to Jack David, publisher and knight in Canadian armor, at ECW Press.

Others who helped me with this book also deserve thanks: Shelly Cofield, Eric Rosen, Dr. Mike Lano, Marco Shark, Dennis Wojtowitz, and the softball boys, Vladimir Abouzeide, Anthony (A.J.) Jackson and John Colon.

Now for the folks in the wrestling business — without whom "Missy Hyatt" would never have existed: John Tatum, David Manning, Fritz Von Erich, Dusty Rhodes, Rick Hazzard, Eddie Gilbert, Paul E. and Ken Resnick. I'd like to thank Mick Foley for writing his book and convincing publishers that wrestling fans do actually read. Last, but not least, I'd like to pay special tribute to Jim Ross. He was the only person in this crazy business who was always on my side; he was my mentor, my shrink, and most importantly my friend. Jim, even if I never said it in words, I hope you know how much your support has meant to me through the years.

Now look: I never kept a journal while I was working in the pro wrestling business, so when the time came to write my memoirs, I had to work from memory. I'm sure there's a lot of stuff I remember differently from other people. Lots of stuff I don't remember at all. Lots of stuff I'd rather not remember. What that means, guys, is that if I left you out, I didn't mean to. Or maybe I did.

Introduction

It makes no sense — I mean, if you stop and think about it.

Two guys beat each other to bloody pulps for half an hour, slugging each other in the face, kicking each other in the groin, banging metal chairs over each other's heads, body-slamming each other through wooden tables, and the crowd just sits on their hands. Like, *Snore!* But then, suddenly, a couple of chicks — I mean "valets" — jump into the ring, grab one another in headlocks, and start rolling around, and now the crowd's on their feet, jumping up and down, climbing onto their chairs, shoving and elbowing for a better view, yelling *Catfight! Catfight! Catfight!*

That's what's about to happen in five minutes. Sandman and Raven are going to knock each other out, a double-clothesline kind of deal; then me and Lori are going to jump into the ring, grab headlocks and roll around. No *problemo*. Done it a hundred times. It's all scripted.

Well, maybe one weensy *problemo*. Me and Lori don't get along too well. That's unusual, in case you're curious. Most of the women I've gotten to know in the business have been real sweethearts. Sunshine, Sunny, Elektra, Baby Doll, Francine, Kimona, Terri Runnels, Lady Blossom. But Lori, she's one of the exceptions.

Back in the dressing room, as we were going over the match, step by step, she was giving me nothing but attitude. She'd already marched herself down the tunnel to Paul E.'s office — that's the promoter — to complain that my outfit was sexier than hers, like if she'd known I was going to wear a sports bra and micro-mini, she wouldn't have worn just a plain old tube top and jeans. Except what can she say? I mean, really. Not to sound stuck up, but I'm Missy. And she's . . . well, she's Lori. That's just how things are.

So we're talking through the moves back in the dressing room, and it's by-the-numbers kind of stuff. I could do it in my sleep. After the double-clothesline, she's going to jump into the ring to revive her guy, Raven, then I'm going to jump in to protect my guy, Sandman, and then I'm going to tackle her, then she's going to get on top of me, then I'm going to kick out from underneath, then more rolling around, me on top of her, her on top of me, back and forth, etc, etc, etc. Finally, since I'm the babyface, I lay her out with a right cross. She winds up stunned in the corner. But then, when I go to revive Sandman, she's supposed to pull off her leather boot, rush up behind me, and knock me out with it.

She hasn't looked me in the eye once, the whole conversation.

"Look," I say, finally, "Just be careful with the boot."

"I know what I'm doing," she shoots back, ice cold.

"What I mean is, don't hit the pony tail."

The reason I'm worried is because I'm wearing a long blond pony tail fall, and if Lori hits me straight on the pony tail, she's going to knock the fall off my head. She's supposed to hit me just in front of the fall, with the soft toe of the boot.

Except now she's got this look on her face, like: *Whatever!*

I guess I should explain that the situation's more complicated than just me and Lori. To start off with, she's working with Raven, and I'm working with Sandman — and the two of them aren't too fond of each other. Raven's about to jump companies from Paul E's Extreme Championship Wrestling to Ted Turner's World Championship Wrestling. Which is like going from a Dodge Dart to a Lincoln Continental. And Sandman figures it should've been him who got the call. So now Raven's scared Sandman's drunk again and might shoot on him — you know, clamp on the holds for real, try to hurt him.

But that's not the end of it.

Lori is Lori Fullington, and Sandman's real name is James Fullington. The two of them are married. Now I'm with Sandman, and Lori's never quite gotten past the fact that Sandman became a headliner with me ringside whereas he was never more than a mid-card guy with her. That, plus she thinks I slept with him. (Not guilty, for just about the only time!)

It's just a mess.

Raven and Lori are already in the ring when Sandman's music comes on: "Enter Sandman" I mean, how original! It's a song by Metallica, a heavy metal group. I liked it maybe the first dozen times I heard it, but now I've heard it about a thousand times, and the guitar intro shoots straight into my brain; it's like an Excedrin Moment.

Say your prayers, every one
Don't forget, my son,
To include everyone . . .

INTRODUCTION

The second I pop my head through the curtains, the Philly crowd goes nuts. Sandman steps through after me, carrying his two trademarks: a Singapore cane and a can of beer. Now he takes the lead, and the two of us start down the aisle towards the ring. The aisle is maybe five feet wide, and fans are leaning over the metal barricade. Half of them are patting him on the back; the other half are trying to cop a feel as I pass by. Security is just a couple of beefy guys from a local motorcycle club; they couldn't care less.

Sandman stops at the edge of the ring, and now the real show begins. He jumps up on the ring apron and goes into his shtick, smashing the can of beer against his forehead over and over until it explodes, and then he shoots beer foam into the first row of fans. They lap it up, literally. It's like a frenzy now; the noise is deafening as Sandman guzzles down the rest of the can. By the time he stops, blood's starting to leak down his forehead. That's part of his gimmick too — Sandman's a bleeder.

Then he reaches down for me. It's like suddenly he's a gentleman, and he's helping me up to the ring. His entire torso is soaked with beer and sweat, and blood is trickling into the corners of his eyes — and the match hasn't even started yet! It kind of grosses me out, to be honest, but I'm used to it, so I take his hand and climb up onto the ring apron. I use my butt to hold down the second rope, then lift up the top rope so Sandman can step into the ring. Then I slide through the ropes myself, real slow, because I know the television camera's zooming in for the panty shot.

That's when the chant starts: *Show your tits! Show your tits! Show your tits!*

As if!

But I tease them for about a few seconds, just to get their hopes up. I glance over at Sandman, you know, as though I'm asking his opinion. Like: *What do you think? Should I go for it?* Then he turns to the crowd and kind of shrugs, like: *Is that what you came to see?*

The crowd starts to chant: *We want tits! We want tits! We want tits!*

So I reach for the sports bra, and I shift it around for a split-second. The crowd is screaming now, not chanting. But then, a split-second later, I flip them the finger. Both hands.

Like I'm going to show them my tits!

Boooooooo!

viii　　　**MISSY HYATT**

Miss York aka Marlena aka Terri Runnels and me on my birthday in Atlanta, 10/92

INTRODUCTION

Me and my hair

The match starts up about a minute later. It goes back and forth between Sandman and the Raven, just like it's supposed to. You'd never know there were hard feelings between them. Finally comes the double-clothesline. Lori jumps in, and I jump in, and we grab each other and start rolling around, and at first I think it's going to be all right between the two of us too. She gets on top of me like she's supposed to and grabs me by the throat.

That's when I feel her nails across the side of my neck.

It's no big deal, just a scratch. It's the kind of thing that happens when you're catfighting. I've done it to other girls myself. You whisper you're sorry, and you keep going. But I get nothing from Lori — except the sense that she's into it. Hurting me, I mean.

"Damn it," I whisper.

I start trying to push her off, but she's still straddling me, still holding tight onto my neck. She's not squeezing — I mean, I can breathe — but she's not letting go either. Finally, I reach up and grab her hair, and then the two of us start rolling around the ring. The thing is, she's still got hold of my throat the entire time.

Finally, I manage to kick her off, and for an instant the two of us are just sitting on our butts, catching out breaths. Then our eyes meet. She looks at me in a strange way, sad, as though she's sorry she got carried away. I think maybe she's back in character.

Then she jumps up and comes at me with the boot.

The timing's all wrong, we're not even half way through our moves, but I jump up and brace for the shot. Instead of the soft toe, though, she smacks me with the heel right on top of the pony tail. As I collapse to the canvas, I can feel the fall flying off my head.

Now I'm lying on the canvas, pretending to be knocked out, and I hear another chant start from the crowd:

Where's your hair?
Where's your hair?
Where's your hair?

I peek out the corner of my eye. The fall is lying like a dead rat in the middle of the ring, right over the C in ECW. It's about six inches from my right hand, just out of reach. I can't grab it without rolling over — which would pretty much kill the illusion that I'm knocked out. I catch sight of Lori. She's leaning against the ropes across the ring; she's staring down at the fall with a look that's a combination of confusion and horror, pure panic. That's bad because she's supposed to react like she just won the catfight. She's supposed to strut around the ring.

For a few seconds, I don't know what to do. The match between Sandman and Raven is technically over; it's a double disqualification because Lori and I jumped into the ring and interfered. The referee has called for the bell. But Sandman and Raven are still lying motionless. Lori's strut is supposed to be the cue for them to stagger to their feet and leave the ring. But she's not strutting, and they're not moving.

Finally, I think to myself: *Is there one person in the entire building who actually believes I'm unconscious?*

So I sit up.

"It's a miracle!" I hear a guy in the front row shout.

I snatch up the fall by the pony tail, and I start waving it at the crowd. They *love it!* Now I'm strutting around the ring, twirling the pony tail over my head, and the crowd is standing and cheering. Then I strut over to Sandman and swat him with it, as if I'm using the pony tail to wake him up, and he opens his eyes and starts to crack up. I hear Raven laughing from across the ring. Even Lori's cracking up.

Back in the dressing room, afterwards, Lori is telling me how sorry she is for what happened. She doesn't mean a word of it; she still hates my guts. We both know it's not over. Not by a long shot. But for now I tell her it's no big deal.

And it isn't really — a big deal, I mean.

Naturally, fifteen years ago, it would have been . . .

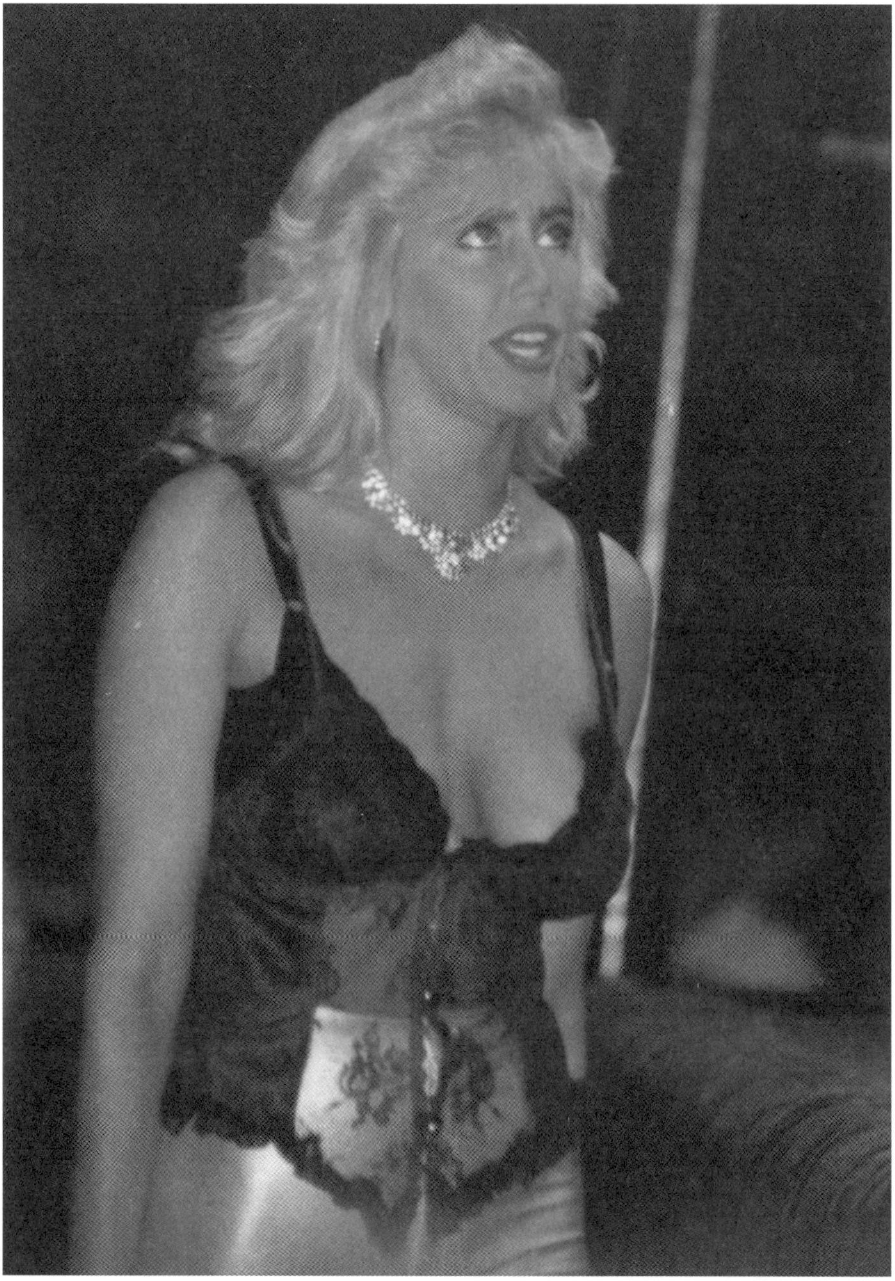

1

Sweet Melissa

Florida and Georgia, unaffiliated

Missy Hyatt was born in Fritz Von Erich's backstage office at the Sportatorium in Dallas, Texas — and if you have to ask who Fritz Von Erich is, then you don't know a thing about Texas wrestling.

So like I was saying, Missy was born in a dingy backstage office at the Sportatorium. The entire room was maybe twelve by twelve, with a metal desk in the middle, and lit by a sixty watt bulb hanging from the ceiling — which, by the way, could have used a good paint job. Lots of shadows, lots of cigarette smoke. And it was packed. Besides Fritz, who was sitting behind the desk in a zippered jump suit, there were his two sons, Kevin and Kerry Von Erich, Rick Hazzard, Ken Mantel, the booker, and John Tatum. And last but not least, there was this wide-eyed chick from Tallahassee, Florida named Melissa Hiatt.

The year was 1985 when Melissa Hiatt walked in, and Missy Hyatt walked out. Missy Hyatt. The First Lady of Professional Wrestling. Spoiled socialite, manipulative maneater, and heiress (so-she-claims) to the Hyatt Hotel fortune.

What a bitch!

Left: My older sister Robin holding me, three months old

Below: "Messy," 1 1/2 years old

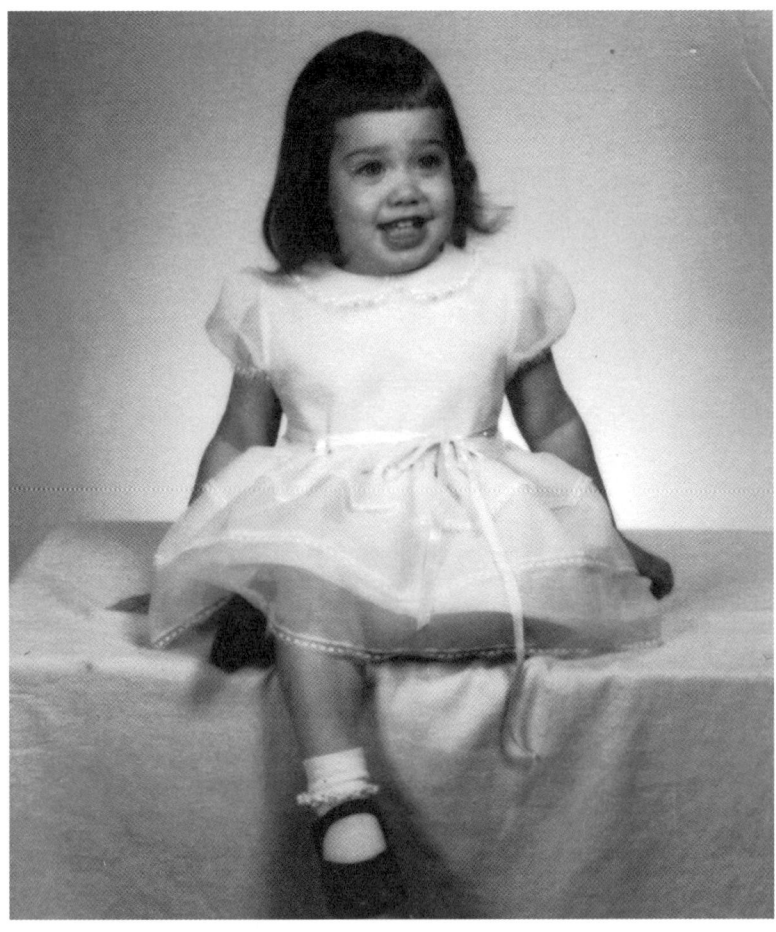

Naturally, like everything else in wrestling, "Missy" is part fantasy, part reality, and no one, not even me, is sure where one ends and the other begins. You could get all intellectual about it — like what's really reality? — but that just makes the entire thing way more serious than it's supposed to be. Pro wrestling is a show, pure and simple. The fans know it. It's like if you're watching a magician saw a lady in half, you know he's not actually sawing her in half. But you sit in the crowd and go with it, you ooh and ahh, because it's fun. Wrestling's like that too. It's entertainment. You just can't take it too seriously.

But getting back to Missy, in order to understand what makes her tick — which I just know you're dying to find out — you've got to know a little about Melissa. Which is who I was. And who I still am, sometimes, if you catch me without makeup.

Melissa Hiatt was born in nineteen-sixty-none-of-your-business. John Kennedy was president . . . and, like Forrest Gump says, *That's all I'm going to say about that.* I grew up in Tallahassee. My dad was a salesman, and my mom was . . . well, a mom. They adopted three girls. Robin, Vonda and me, in that order. Comfortable, middle-class house. Robin died of mononucleosis when she was sixteen. I was six years old at the time, so I don't remember a lot about Robin.

As for being adopted, I know that's like, you know, an issue for lots of people. But not for me. I was raised knowing I was adopted. And the thing is, if I would have had a zillion parents to choose from, and they all turned in references and resumes and stuff, I couldn't have picked a better mom and dad than the ones I wound up with. That's boring, I suppose. I know you guys want the dirt. Well, the only bad relationship I can remember from my childhood was with Robin's chihuahua, Buddy. That little guy hated me! From the day my parents brought me home, Buddy just couldn't stand me. Even my mother knew it. She said that when she would change my diaper, Buddy would sometimes jump up onto the bed and pee on my clothes. I guess I must have tormented him — I mean, I was the baby of the family, the youngest by eight years, so who else was I going to pick on except the dog?

After Robin passed away, Buddy ran off and never came back. My

On my motorcycle

folks put up fliers, searched the entire neighborhood for him. A friend of mine who's married to a vet once told me that dogs mourn for the people they love, and I believe it. As soon as Robin was gone, that dog just picked up and left. We never saw him again.

Kind of sad.

High school was when I first figured out something about myself, something that's kind of stuck with me ever since: I didn't give a rat's ass what other people thought about me. Maybe it was a reaction, a self-defense kind of thing, since I didn't fit in. In my school, you were either an Archie or a Freak. The Archies, they were like yuppies-in training. They wore Izods, you know, alligator-patch shirts and jackets, and straight-legged

Levi's. Then you had the Freaks, kids who smoked dope and hung out on the corner in Wrangler jeans; the guys wore tie-dyes and the girls wore tube tops.

I suppose, if I had to choose one, I would've been a freak — mainly because I liked Wranglers better than Levis. But the marijuana, the way the smell got in your clothes and hair, it was like, Ugh. So, basically, I just went my own way. Which pissed off both groups. So, yeah, I used to get teased. I'd be walking down the hallway on my way to class, and I'd hear people snickering. That kind of stuff. But then, years later, after I was doing the first TBS wrestling show, I'd go home and visit my folks, and those same people would come up to me in Walmart, and suddenly they're like, "Hey, Missy, remember me? Beth Ann! We took eleventh grade English together. I sat in the row behind you." And then I'm like, "Let me think . . . Beth Ann . . . Beth Ann . . . no, doesn't ring a bell. Nothing's coming to me. But, hey, do you want me to autograph that box of Pampers?"

But I'm always extra nice to little kids. I'll stoop over and pick them up, or else I'll kneel down and talk to them eye to eye. It always pays to be nice to kids. And also to the people who work the drive through window at Burger King. 'Cause if you're not, they'll spit in your Whopper.

So I didn't dress like an Archie, and I didn't dress like a Freak. Clothes-wise, I think the only goal I had when I left the house every morning was to look older than I was. I remember there was this girl, Vicki Ridner, and she was the hottest chick in the entire school. She had long blond hair, and she got all the attention from the guys. That was what made me decide to bleach my hair. I knew my parents would never cough up the money to have it done professionally. So I figured I'd do it myself. I waited until my folks weren't home, and then I tried pouring bleach on my head. I mean laundry bleach. What did I know? I must have been fifteen years old! Well, that didn't work — it just reeked — so then I went and bought a box of blonde hair dye. But my hair was so dark, the dye turned it a kind of dull orange. Then I *had* to go and get it fixed in a salon because my folks didn't want me walking around with orange hair.

That's how I became a blond.

Now the thing about being a blond is you've got to be able to carry it off. Blond is more than a hair color, you know? It's an attitude. It took a couple of weeks for the blond to work its way into my attitude. But once it did, watch out! I was fifteen, and I ruled the world.

Searching for just the right look

What shocks lots of people is that I wasn't a big wrestling fan as a kid. No one in my house watched it on television. Still, I knew who Dusty Rhodes was — because back then he was kind of like God in Florida. His posters were up in store windows. He was easy to recognize.

One Saturday afternoon, when I was seventeen, I came home from the mall, walked upstairs, and I remember turning towards my room. But then, as I leaned into my parents' bedroom to say hey to my dad, something caught my eye. My dad was flipping past channels during the commercial of an old movie he was watching. What was on the TV screen at that split-second was wrestling. I didn't know it at the time, but it was Georgia Championship Wrestling. The guys on camera were the Fabulous Freebirds and Michael Hayes. I had no idea who they were, but the angle they were playing just got to me. Hayes and Buddy Roberts were tying a baby bonnet on Bam Bam Gordy's head, then sticking a plastic bottle in his mouth. I mean, it was such a hoot! Gordy was this gigantic guy with long curly brown hair and a huge gut, and he was standing in the middle of the ring sucking on a baby bottle!

My dad was about to change the channel again, but I yelled at him, "No, wait! Wait!"

He just glanced back at the television and said, "What?"

Then I'm like, "This is so cool!"

He just stared at me as if I'd lost my mind. Which, in a way, I had. Because I was hooked. It wasn't the wrestling that got to me. It was the show, the spectacle. The crowd was howling and laughing and applauding, and Hayes and Roberts were jumping up and down, running in circles, pointing at Bam Bam, and it was just a *sight*.

My dad never did catch the end of that movie because I forced him to sit through the rest of the wrestling program with me. And I knew, by the end of the hour, that I wanted to be part of it. No, that I was going to be part of it. I had no clue how because I sure didn't want to be a wrestler. But I was like a little kid who goes to the circus with his folks and afterwards says to himself, "That's the life for me." It's not as if he has a definite plan at that moment; he just *knows*. Whatever it takes, that's what he'll do. Like, *You want to shoot me out of the cannon? Sure, I'll do that.*

With the Geiser Gang

SWEET MELISSA

There are two kinds of people who follow wrestling. People who know that the matches are fixed; and people who feel like they have to tell you the matches are fixed. I mean, it's impossible not to know. I think if you brought a near-sighted dolphin to the arena, even he'd know the matches were fixed. I remember one time, around 1990 or '91, I was sitting in an airport lounge in Dallas, drinking a Diet Coke, and this suit slides a chair up next to mine. Now I'm really not in the mood for this; my flight's already delayed two hours; plus, I'm PMS-ing off the chart. But I figure it's the kind of situation that comes with the territory, so I smile at the guy.

"You're Missy," he says.

"That's right."

"You're the one on TBS."

"That's me."

There's a long pause, real awkward.

Then, finally, he says, "That wrestling shit is so fake. I always know who's going to win."

Well, duh!

Normally, I just shrug off that sort of remark, you know, just keep smiling and nodding my head. But, like I said, I'm running two hours late, and I'm PMS-ing, and there's something about this guy, about the way he pulled up his chair without asking first, about how he's leaning with his elbows on the table, about how he's grinning at me, that just gets under my skin.

"Look," I said, "Did you see *Indiana Jones*?"

"Yeah."

"Did you really think that boulder was chasing Harrison Ford down the freaking hill?"

"No."

"Did you see *Top Gun*?"

"Yeah."

"Did you really think Tom Cruise was flying that freaking jet fighter?"

"Well, no."

"Then why the *fuck* do you find it necessary to tell me wrestling is fake?"

MISSY HYATT

*From geek to clown . . .
see – there's hope for everyone*

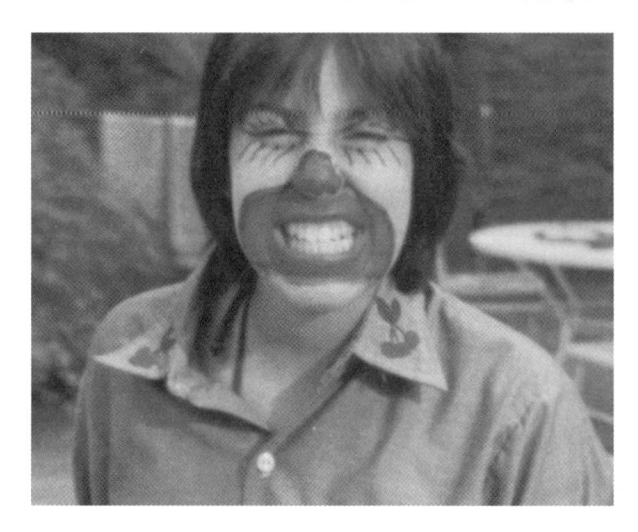

He let out kind of a soft laugh, stood up and sort of slinked away. I felt bad about it afterwards; actually, I still do. I mean, he was just a lonely guy in an airport making conversation. Probably didn't know what else to say. So if you're reading this, Mr. Suit, I apologize.

It was the bogus part of wrestling, the soap opera angles, that first intrigued me when I started to follow it on television. I didn't have a favorite wrestler back then; I just loved the storylines, the way the announcers would give certain guys a push — how they'd build them up by inventing colorful backgrounds.

Back in those days, the early 1980's, the TV tapings were mostly squash matches — a headliner against a jobber. You knew what was happening from the start of the program, when the announcers were running down the card, because one of them would say, "And later on in the hour, we've got the young stallion, Tommy Wildfire Rich, a real up and comer, a future champion, and he'll be going up against . . . wait, let me see, it's Tommy Wildfire Rich against Joe Blow." The jobber's job was to make the headliner look good. Back then, headliners never wrestled against each other on television. The major matches were saved for the house shows. In a way, the television tapings were like infomercials for the next house show. The headliners would wrestle the jobbers on TV, and in between matches, during the interviews, there would be like a half-minute confrontation between the headliner who had just won his match and the headliner who was about to wrestle. The two of them would lunge at one another and be held back, and then one of them would yell, "You got lucky tonight! But just wait till I get you in the ring in Atlanta on the 23rd!"

The first wrestler I singled out, by the way, was Tommy Wildfire Rich. He was like the number one babyface with Georgia Championship Wrestling. I remember how the TV camera would cut to him driving up to the arena in a blue Trans Am — and, at the time, I was driving a gold Trans Am. Plus, he had long bleached-blonde hair, and so did I — we had like so much in common — and he would stare into the camera and talk straight to the women in the audience, like, "Hey, darlin'".

It just melted me.

So I turned eighteen, and then I heard about another girl at school

Ruling the world as a blond

who liked wrestling named Dana. I barely knew who she was; I just remembered that she was real tall and kind of plain-looking. Like that kind of Kansas face. Well, it turned out that Dana was crazy in love with a wrestler named Barry Windham, and she used to drive to the Florida shows to watch him. So one afternoon I called her up out of the blue, and at first I had to explain who I was, but then we started to talk about wrestling, and we kind of bonded, and then, finally, I said, "Let's go to the matches next week." She wanted to go to a local show in Tallahassee, but those weren't the wrestlers I wanted to see — I wanted to see Tommy Wildfire Rich and the Freebirds with Georgia Championship Wrestling — so we talked back and forth, and finally, after a half hour, she gave in. I think she was just happy to have a friend to sit beside at the matches.

The next Georgia Championship Wrestling show was on a Wednesday night in Macon — 200 miles north of Tallahassee. Dana and I cut school and started out at about nine in the morning, and we arrived so early — like five hours before the matches started. So we were waiting out in the parking lot, just kind of hanging around, doing nothing. I guess we were sort of hoping one of the wrestlers would drive up. I remember I had on a pair of real tight Sergio Valente jeans, the kind where you had to lay down on a bed and pull them up over your thighs and butt with a special metal hook. (Stop smiling! It was the early eighties!) I think I was wearing a tee shirt or maybe a sleeveless blouse. Nothing too revealing. But I do think I had on high heel, fuck-me pumps, so I'm pretty sure I looked older than eighteen.

Maybe an hour later, a middle-aged man drove up. He didn't tell us his name, but he told us he was one of the promoters — actually, he might have been just a maintenance worker since he rolled into the lot in a banged up old Civic. If he was a promoter, he certainly wasn't the main guy. But he noticed us hanging around in front of the ticket window, like we were a two-person line, waiting for someone to show up and sell us tickets. He walked over and started to talk to us, asked us who we came to see. So I blurted out, "Oh my God, I want to meet Tommy Wildfire Rich. It's my first wrestling match."

He just kind of smiled at us and nodded. Then he headed through a side door and into the arena. The two of us watched him walk inside, waited for something to happen, but nothing did. So we waited another couple of hours until the ticket lady turned up. We bought ringside tickets because we were the first on line, but then, when the doors finally opened up, we kind of got elbowed out of the way and wound up in the fifth row. It didn't matter to us though; we were psyched just to be there.

Except then, just as we were settling into our seats, the guy from the parking lot turned up again and told us to come with him. He ducked us under the aisle ropes and led us down to two seats in the front row; then he just disappeared again. Like I said, we never even found out his name. But we were squealing and jumping up and down like the girls in the Ed Sullivan audience when the Beatles played. I mean, the whole thing was just so geeky.

Finally, the matches started, and the two of us were into it like you wouldn't believe. Whistling at the babyfaces. Hooting at the heels. After about an hour, it's time for Tommy Rich's match. He's strutting down the aisle, and I'm like shaking because he's so close. Then, suddenly, he stops right in front of me and Dana, squeezes in between us, and he drapes his arms over our shoulders — the guy from the parking lot must have described us and mentioned the crush I had on him. Then Dana whips out her camera and snaps a picture of me and Tommy Rich. (I kept that photograph for years, but I think John Tatum burned it after I left him.) Then, just as Tommy's about to climb into the ring, I looked him straight in the eyes and said, "I hope you kick Michael Hayes's butt!"

Just like a mark!

After the matches, I wound up riding around with Tommy in his car — just driving around and around, with Dana following us in her car. Tommy's trying to talk me into giving him a blow job. I'm kind of giggling and shaking my head. But the truth is, I know I'm going to do it. Finally, we stopped at a red light, he slid his arm around my shoulder and said, "C'mon, darlin'!"

The thing I remember is Dana honking her horn behind us as the light changed to green and then back to red about three times.

From that night on, I was a wrestling-junkie. Couldn't get enough. Dana and I started going to every wrestling show we could drive to, and when Dana wasn't around, I went on my own. To give you an idea what kind of maniac I was, I'd sometimes watch the same show three times. Remember, in those days, the house shows were never televised. So the promoters would schedule the exact same card, the exact same matches, in three different cities. I'd drive to all three, watch the wresters run through the same sequence of holds — and I loved it. Sometimes, if Dana was with me, we'd start predicting out loud what was about to happen in the ring. Then it would happen, and whoever was sitting around us would be like, "Hey, you guys must know something." Then we'd be like, "Oh, yeah, we know the wrestlers. We hang out with them after the show."

Naturally, I got to know other fans. Wrestling fans are kind of like Deadheads, the people who used to follow the Grateful Dead from concert to concert. It's a traveling community. And, yes, wrestlers do have groupies. They're called Arena Rats. Or at least that's what the wrestlers call them. Except for that first time with Tommy Wildfire Rich, I was never a real Arena Rat, but I guess I was kind of a small mouse.

Besides getting to know other fans, I also started to recognize the promoters. Dory Funk was one of them. And then, one day, Dory Funk's girlfriend came up to me outside an arena in Florida and asked me to sell programs. So that was my first "in."

Eventually, the wrestlers themselves started to recognize me. They'd wave to me on their way into the arena. Nothing more than that. I was nineteen at that point, out of high school, and I'd been on the house show circuit for almost two years.

It was in Columbus, Georgia, that I met this girl named Cheryl. Dana wasn't with me, and Cheryl and I began to talk outside the arena. She was a pretty girl; she had a body like a dancer's. Blond hair. Green eyes. She said she lived in Atlanta, and I said, "Wow, that's where all the wrestlers live!" Then she mentioned that she'd dated some of them, and she told me lots of gossip. I was in heaven. Cheryl and I became friends, and I ended up moving in with her about a month later. And then, *oh my God!*, she would have wrestlers coming in and out of the apartment all the time.

That's where I met Jake Roberts.

Jake Roberts was the first wrestler I ever dated. It lasted less than a year, but he was a *major* character! Actually, "character" is the nicest way to put it. He was flat out weird.

Cheryl introduced me to him. She and I were at the Omni in Atlanta, sitting in the section for friends and guests of the wrestlers — because, like I said, Cheryl knew just about everyone. Jake walked by on the way to the ring, and the two of us made eye contact. It was just a split second kind of thing. But he smiled at me, and I smiled back at him. Cheryl noticed it, and she elbowed me in the ribs. Then, after the show, Jake jogged up behind us in the parking lot to talk to Cheryl. Except not really. It was sweet, the way he did it.

And, *no*, he didn't work with a snake back then!

Being Jake's girlfriend was an experience. I mean, in some ways it was great. Like I'd drive up to the arenas before his matches, and I'd give my name to the security guard, and he'd nod, and I'd walk right on in. Right past the line of fans. I knew them too, the fans on line; I used to be one of them. And I'd glance back at them, like, *Yeah, right, I'm Jake's girlfriend now. And you're still standing on line, still elbowing each other for the good seats.* I was a snot, no doubt about it.

But in other ways, being his girlfriend was just plain weird. There's no other word for it. He had this thing he liked to do at bars. He'd send me in, alone, to sit at the bar, and he'd wait outside. He'd hang around on the sidewalk and peer inside through the window, and wait until some guy slid onto the next stool and started to hit on me. Then he'd strut through the door, so that the entire place noticed him except for the guy talking to me at the bar, and he'd come up behind the two of us. What he liked was the look on the guy's face when he glanced over his shoulder. There'd be Jake, who was like six-foot-four, and the guy would turn around and then crane his neck up to look him in the eyes. Then Jake would be like, "That's my woman you're talking to." He'd scare the poor guy half-to-death. Jake never laid a hand on one of them, mind you, but the entire scene always struck me as kind of psycho.

Another thing he liked to do — and I know it's going to sound funny — was play gin rummy. It's funny, I know, because he doesn't seem like the type; I mean, one night he'd want to go out and intimidate guys in bars and the next he'd want to stay home and play 500 rummy. Hand after hand, round after round — literally, we'd play all night. We'd run through about ten pages of scratch paper keeping score and still be going at it.

Hey, I was so naïve, I didn't realize what was going on for like three months. I just figured the guy just loved to play cards.

But all the sleepless nights had nothing to do with card games. It was the cocaine, naturally.

Now it's no secret in the wrestling world that Jake's always had problems with drugs and alcohol. He's kind of a tragic figure because, as far as wrestling was concerned, he had the whole package. The look. The size. The brains. The charisma. He could talk. He could wrestle. He could work as a babyface or as a heel. Lots of people think he might have wound up as big as Hulk Hogan. But he could never stay clean.

The first time I did coke was with Jake; it's not something I'm proud of, but it happened. We were at a club called Shenanigans in Atlanta, and suddenly he grabbed me by the hand and said, "C'mon." Then he led me out into the parking lot; I had no clue why; I thought maybe he wanted to go home, or else he wanted a blow job (which, in a way, he did). So we walked out into the parking lot, and Jake reached into his shirt pocket and pulled out a plastic spoon.

"What?" I said. "You got yogurt?"

He just started to laugh.

Then he pulled out the baggie.

I confess: I was curious. I did one snort and didn't feel a thing. The two of us walk back into the club, and I'm thinking, *That's what it's like? I mean, big whoop!* But then, a couple of minutes later, I felt like dancing. Which was strange since before Jake dragged me out to the parking lot, I was pooped and kind of ready to go home. Next thing I know, I'm dancing with about a dozen different guys. I mean, all at once. Then I'm running around the bar, striking up conversations with strangers. Not just guys. Chicks. Couples. Most of them can't even hear me over the music; they're just grinning and nodding their heads, but I'm so into these five-minute conversations. I'm pounding on the bar, arguing with myself, and I can't seem to make people understand how important what I'm talking about is. Whatever the hell it is I'm talking about. Because I can't remember what I'm talking about from one conversation to the next.

It's frustrating the crap out of me!

Finally, I feel Jake's hand on my wrist. It pisses me off at first, you know, because it feels like I've just started to get to the point I've been trying to make all night. But then I glance back around, and the people I was just talking to are gone. So Jake leads me to the bathroom, and he splashes water in my face and stands me up in front of the mirror.

I mean, I had like hamster-eyes. You know what I mean? Where your eyeballs look like they're going to pop out of their sockets and roll down your cheeks.

Then he gave me halcion, and I slept for two days.

Jake was more than just a wrestler. He was also one of the two main bookers for the organization — the other was Bob Roop. They scripted the storylines and match ups. The entire time I was going out with Jake, he was telling me, "Oh, don't worry, we'll come up with a gimmick for you. Trust me, you're going to be great."

Truthfully, I was nervous at first. The thought of actually climbing into the ring, of doing an angle in front of a crowd . . . I kept telling Jake I was happy just being his girlfriend. But he knew it was what I wanted in my heart, and he kept egging me on. He told me about an organization in Texas, World Class Championship Wrestling, that was doing angles with valets. They had two at that point, Sunshine and Precious. Jake knew they

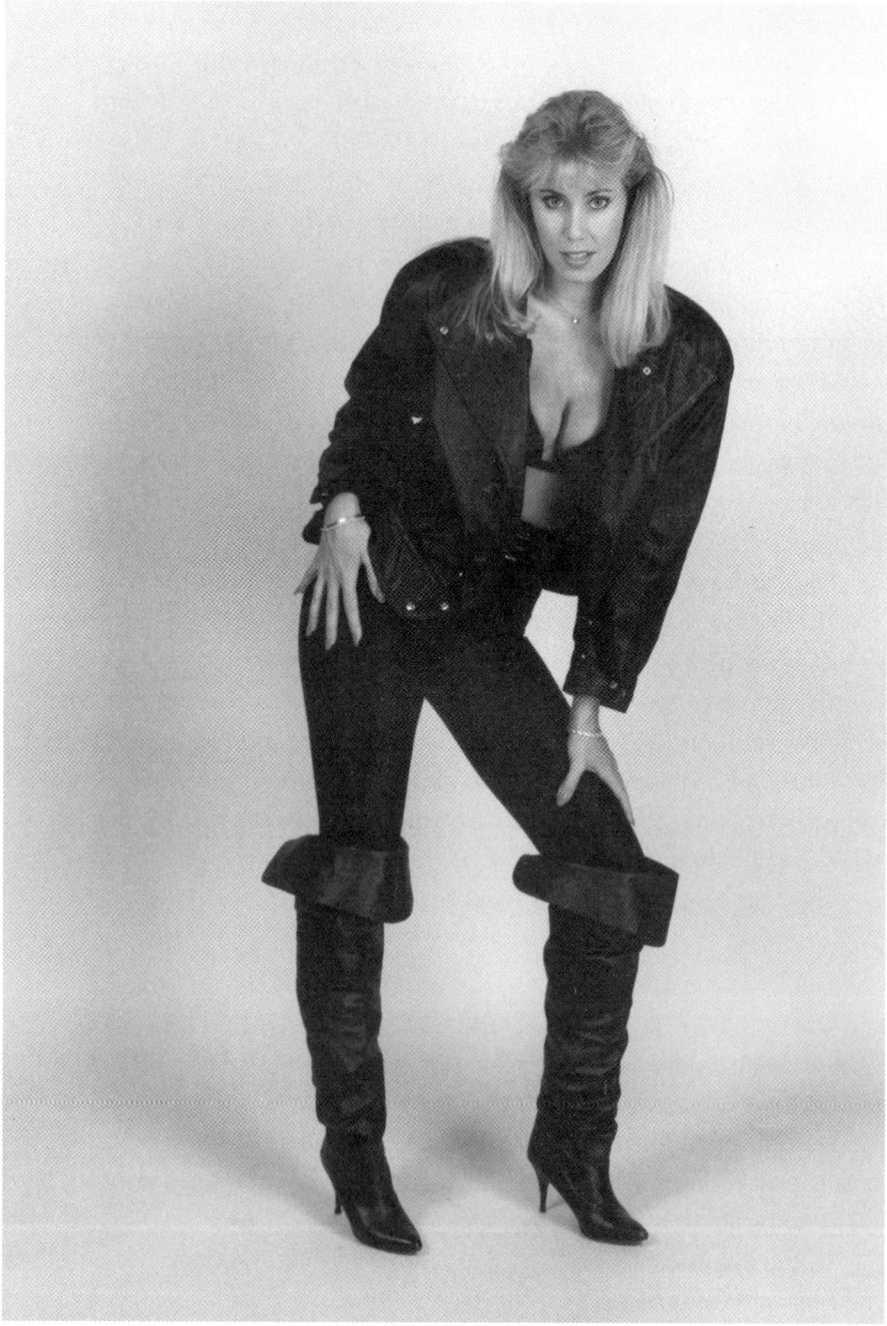

were looking for a third, and he told me to go for it. But I didn't want to split up with Jake, and I kind of dragged my feet, and just when I'd made up my mind to call, I found out another girl, Baby Doll, got the gig.

I was real depressed about it for a couple of weeks, so Jake and Bob were determined to work out an angle for me in Georgia. Finally, Bob came up with the idea of putting me inside a box and giving me to Jake in the ring — you know, like a present before his match. Jake was going to untie the pink ribbon, pull open the box, and then I'd pop out. Except instead of giving him a big kiss, I was going to turn on him and start hitting him with my shoe. Then he'd DDT me — yank me down head first into the mat. And afterwards, I'd be out for revenge.

But the idea never got off the drawing board. Jake was afraid people would see us together outside the arena — since we were dating, I mean. I know it sounds silly that he'd be worried about that. But in those days, you tried to keep up the illusion. Babyfaces and heels couldn't even have dinner together after the matches.

One thing about wrestling that's very different nowadays is the attitude of the fans. It's not like the fans back in the 1980's thought the matches were on the level; it's just that they bought into the storylines. I had a professor a couple of semesters ago who talked about *suspension of disbelief* — that's when you know what's going on isn't real, but you play along. Fans were willing to play along fifteen years ago. Now, with all the wrestling hotlines and internet reports, you hear things in the crowd like, "So-and-so's getting a major push in the organization" and "That guy's contract is up next month, so he's going to have to lose the belt."

The ironic thing is that the angle with me going off on Jake would have worked because he broke up with me about a month later . . . so it wouldn't have been a problem not being seen together.

I guess I didn't take the break up well; it was like a personal crisis. His best friend was Road Warrior Hawk, and a week after Jake dumped me, I slept with Hawk just to get back at him.

Then I got a boob job.

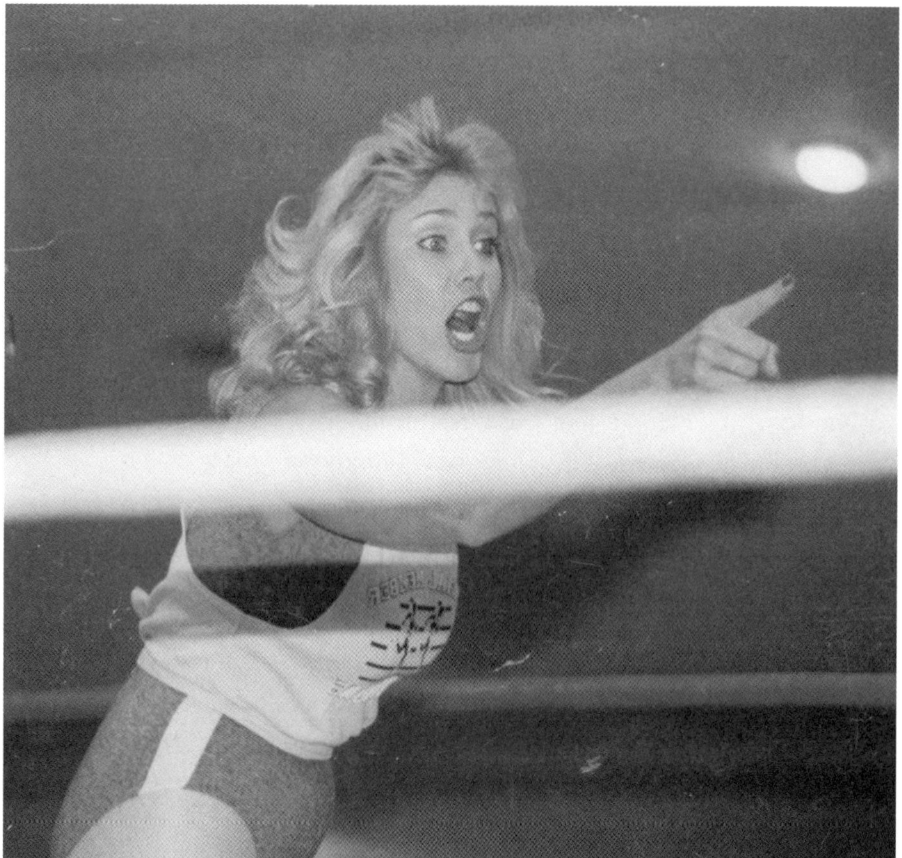

2

Learning the Ropes

Dallas, WCCW

It was about a year after Jake was out of the picture that Cheryl introduced me to John Tatum. I was running food in a local bar to pay my half of the rent, and I was bored. Then one weekend, Cheryl and I were invited to a cookout at an apartment complex where lots of wrestlers lived. I noticed John lying out by the pool; he had bleached blond hair (notice a pattern?), and he was tall and handsome, and then Cheryl whispered in my ear that he was Jewish, so that clinched it.

When John and I started to date, he was a nobody in the wrestling world. He'd just started out, wrestled a few independent shows. He was making more money golfing than wrestling — I mean, this guy could've been a pro golfer. He'd hustle a couple of marks for eighteen holes in the morning and then work a match at the arena that night.

Actually, I think in his heart John would've rather been a golfer than a wrestler. But it takes beaucoup bucks to join the golf tour — which he didn't have, so he stuck with wrestling. He wasn't a great worker, but he had the size and great facial expressions, and eventually he got a call from Jim Crockett to come join Mid-Atlantic Wrestling up in Charlotte, North Carolina.

John was doing all right in Mid-Atlantic. He was a "hand" — a guy who was being groomed for bigger things. He'd squash the jobbers on television, but then he'd lose to the babyface in the house show. John's major drawback was that he couldn't talk. He sounded like he had a mouthful of marbles, almost like he was drunk, so he couldn't do long interviews. That limited him. Because if you can't talk, you can't hype your matches. That meant that he would never get a push.

That's why it was kind of a shock when Rick Hazzard called from World Class Championship Wrestling. He was helping book there, and he wanted John to come to Texas and work mid-card matches. Rick and John were old friends from Atlanta, and he was just helping out a pal.

It was a definite step up. WCCW was run by Fritz Von Erich, who was kind of a legend in the business. He was known to look after his wrestlers, to develop their characters. Plus, their television cards were syndicated throughout the country, even overseas. It was a no-brainer to take the job.

Plus, WCCW was working angles with valets. I mean, I had no clue if another slot would open up for me, but it certainly crossed my mind. Meanwhile, I figured I'd signed up for courses at a local community college to pass the time.

So I followed John to Texas, and we settled into an apartment in Denton, just north of Dallas. The first night in the new place, I killed a palmetto bug the size of my fist.

It was about a month after John and I moved to Texas that I read in an industry newsletter that the World Wrestling Federation — Vince McMahon's company — was looking for a girl. She was going to be a valet for the Macho Man, Randy Savage.

Now at the time, I was shining boots at a country and western bar. It was around when *Urban Cowboy* was the big movie, so guys would line up to get their boots polished. The thing was, I was awful at it; I'd use the wrong color and slosh polish on the guys' pants. But I wore tank tops and shorts, and I bent over real low, so I was making pretty decent money.

Still, it wasn't exactly the kind of life I'd dreamed of. So when I heard the WWF wanted a girl, I sent my picture in the mail. Just a picture and a note. I didn't think much of anything would come of it. I didn't know a single person in New York at that time; I didn't even mention to John that I was doing it. I just sent in the photo and forgot about it.

Maybe a week later, I got a call from George Scott, the booker with the WWF. We spoke on the phone for half an hour; nothing definite came out of the conversation. He just told me they were looking for a valet for Savage, and he and Vince liked my look. He said they were talking to a couple of other girls, but I was being considered.

As it turned out, I didn't get the job since Savage ended up convincing Vince McMahon to hire his wife Elizabeth to be his valet; I mean, I wasn't going to get that job regardless. But Fritz didn't know that, and when John mentioned to him that I was being considered, he called a meeting in his backstage office at the Sportatorium. It was him, Rick Hazzard, Fritz's sons Kerry and Kevin, John and me. I was nervous, nervous, nervous. I remember my eyes kept blurring. I knew why I was there; John had clued me in ahead of time. But inside the office the entire moment felt surreal, like it wasn't happening. Or like it wasn't happening to me.

As soon as we were all sitting down, Fritz looked up at me. He wasn't smiling or frowning. Just a blank expression. He was this big bald guy in a zippered jump suit; his face was like a sandbag, all lumpy and scarred from when he wrestled. He stared at me for about three seconds and then said, "We're going to give John a valet."

I nodded my head, like it wasn't a big deal.

"You can help him out with interviews. We'll do promos with the two of you. That sound all right?"

I nodded again.

No one mentioned money. I just figured I was going to get paid on the house; like everyone else at the time, how much I made depended on how many people came to the shows I worked. But I didn't care about money. Right then, I was like that kid who wanted to join the circus.

Then Fritz leaned forward across his desk. "So what do we call you?"

The first name that came to mind, and I still don't know why, was "Constance." As soon as it came out of my mouth, it sounded stupid. I mean, *Constance!* Fritz said it to himself a couple of times. He was thinking it over. I was praying he wouldn't like it.

Then John started laughing and said, "Aw, Missy, you can do better than that."

None of them had ever heard John call me Missy before. He introduced me as "Melissa." But John was the only person who still called me Missy.

Fritz began to smile. "Missy?"

Hey, I was so glad not to wind up as *Constance* that I said real quick, "Works for me."

"Why not just use her real name?" John said. "Missy Hiatt."

Then I came up with a twist. Instead of spelling the last name, "Hiatt," which was hard to remember, we'd spell it *Hyatt*. Like the hotel. That way, it would be easier to recognize. Then that led to the idea that the Missy character would be rich — you know, heiress to the hotel fortune. The more we talked about it, you know, brainstorming, the more it fit together. I was going to be a different kind of valet. The rest of girls supported their wrestlers no matter what, yelled encouragements to them at ringside; they were kind of submissive, like cheerleaders. But I was going to be mean. The Spoiled Socialite who was only in it for the fame and the spotlight. I wouldn't be supportive; I just wanted the championship belt. So whenever John would lose, I'd be pissed.

I remember the first night I worked. The angle was to develop a feud with Sunshine — who had just kicked Precious's ass, so she was the number one valet. Plus, she was a babyface, and the Missy character was supposed to be more of a heel, so it was a natural marriage. A match was set up with John against Scott Casey, who was Sunshine's guy. Towards the end, Casey dragged John to the ropes, and Sunshine rushed over and slapped him across the face.

The match ended in a draw. The time limit expired, but as soon as the bell rang, John grabbed the microphone away from the ring announcer, pointed at Sunshine and said, "This thing's between me and your man. You keep your hands off me, lady!" It was like the longest speech John could get out without garbling up the words.

So Sunshine hears this, and she walks right up to him and slaps him across the face again.

"So that's the way you want it?" John says. Then he calls out, "Missy!"

For a couple of seconds, nothing happens. The fans start glancing all around. They don't know what "Missy" means. I mean, as far as the crowd is concerned, John could be calling out a Doberman Pincher. Meanwhile, Scott Casey and Sunshine are right outside the ring; they've got their backs to the aisle, so they don't notice when I strut through the curtains. But the crowd does. They go crazy, hooting and whistling — I'm wearing these pink and white jogging shorts and a tight white shirt. Meanwhile, Casey and Sunshine kind of look at each other like, *What's going on?*

But, of course, neither of them turns around. Not as I'm jogging up the aisle, not as I'm sneaking up behind Sunshine.

Then, finally, Sunshine turns around.

Whack!

I clobber her with my Gucci purse.

I lay her out, and then John clotheslines Scott Casey and lays him out, and then the two of us strut back down the aisle and disappear behind the curtain.

And the feud's on.

Part of the reason the Sunshine/Missy feud clicked better than Sunshine's feuds with Precious or Baby Doll was size, plain and simple. Precious was a little girl, maybe five foot two; Sunshine was like a head taller, so their catfights always looked out of whack. Baby Doll was just the opposite. She was too big, almost six feet tall, so the match up against Sunshine still looked uneven.

The advantage I had was that Sunshine and I were just about the same size, five eight, with big boobs and bleached blond hair. She was rounder in the waist and butt, but whenever we worked together she wore loose-fitting clothes. It was close enough to look balanced.

Right off, Sunshine took me under her wing. You'd think there would be tension, but as soon as Fritz introduced us, she went out of her way to tutor me. I mean, she was just the sweetest girl. I guess part of it was that she was relieved to have someone her own size to work with. It might not seem like a big deal, but it meant the two of us could work in flats. With Sunshine versus Precious or Sunshine versus Baby Doll, one of them always had to wear high heels to make the catfights look fair. That was dangerous. The girl in heels had to be careful not to sprain an ankle. And the girl in flats had to be careful she didn't get gashed by a wayward high heel.

The first set of television interviews I did were terrifying. John and I would walk over to the promo area, and then he'd just stand there, rehearsing his mean look, and then suddenly the camera would swing around to me, and then I'd get the cue to start: "Okay, Missy, it's a thirty second spot for Saturday night in Amarillo. John versus Scott Casey. You're in his corner. Sunshine is in Casey's corner. And three, two, one . . . GO!"

As soon as the red light on the camera clicked on, I fell into character. I began to whine and moan about how Sunshine had touched my man. It was all ad lib: "You know, I cannot believe that Sunshine touched my guy! You are not anybody who touches my guy. I am Missy. You don't have as much class as I have. You're a low class disrespectful bimbo! And Saturday night in Amarillo, I'm going to teach you the meaning of respect."

Then I'd hear, "All right, that's good for Amarillo. Now another for Lubbock, Thursday night. Thirty seconds. And three, two, one . . . GO!"

"Sunshine, it's going to be you and me in Lubbock on Thursday night, and I'm going to teach you the meaning of the word respect. Because you're nothing but a low class bimbo! You don't have the education that I do. You learned everything you know in trailer parks while I was going to the finest boarding schools in New England. Thursday night in Lubbock, I'm going to give you the education you never got."

The feud with Sunshine was the main angle I worked when I started out with WCCW, but there was still a lot of the Missy persona left to develop. I mean, I couldn't define the entire character against Sunshine. Since I was going to be ringside whenever John wrestled, and since it wasn't always going to be against Scott Casey and Sunshine, I had to *do* something.

I had to *be* Missy.

The first thing I had to do was practice looking bored. It's kind of like being a stage actor. If you're bored in real life, you might just turn your head and yawn. But if you want the fans in the back row to see it, you've got to pat your mouth a couple of times and stretch out your arms. I'd do that during the slow moments in John's matches, like when he had his opponent hooked up in a leg lock or something. The fans get bored with that kind of stuff too, so they started to watch me to see how I would react. And I was like, *Ho, hum, boring, can you just finish the guy off already?*

That was when the match was going John's way. But I had to come up with shtick for when John was getting the crap beat out of him. That reaction was especially important since it was what separated me from the other valets — who would keep cheering for their guys, encouraging them to break the holds they were caught in. But that wasn't what Missy would do. Whenever John got in trouble, I would turn my back. Then, after a few seconds, I'd start insulting the fans in the first row. Like I would pick out a fat woman in a pink dress, and I'd start pointing at her and laughing, or I'd find a grungy-looking old man, you know, a hillbilly type, and I'd point him out and then make a motion with my finger as if I were brushing my teeth.

That was just the first bit. I came up with the idea to bring a nail file with me to the ring — so when things weren't going John's way, I'd not only turn my back but also file my nails. I mean, it was all ad lib, all the time. But then I'd think about it afterwards and get another idea. So instead of the nail file, I'd come to the ring with a compact and start to powder my face. Then I added lipstick to that; I wound up re-doing my entire makeup ringside. The crowd ate it up. I was getting booed more than John was.

The next idea I got was to demand a chair. After the introductions, I would climb down through the ropes, look around, and then I'd make John stop his pre-match warm-ups and pull out a folding chair for me from underneath the ring. Then, after we did that a couple of times, John would pull out a chair . . . and I'd shake my head. Like, *No, that chair's not good enough. I want THAT one!* Then I'd point to a fan in the front row, and John would force him to stand up and give me his chair. Then I started to do it to the ring announcers. I'd make John take away their chairs. I used to pull that on Marc Lowrance all the time.

The crowds couldn't *stand* me!

I mean, *wow*, was I getting heat back then. The booing I expected, I wanted, but not the physical stuff. One time, at the Sportatorium, a little old lady caught me in the back of the head with her purse as I was walking down the aisle towards the ring. She was this sweet little thing, like seventy-five years old, not even five feet tall, and she slipped right between two beefy security guys and clocked me.

Another time, at a show in Fort Worth, I got jumped from behind by a group of fans. There were about a half dozen of them. They came over the railing, under the ropes; they had me on the ground. I mean, I was ducking my head, covering up. It was about ten seconds before security pulled them off me. I've had people spit at me, pour beer on me, fling nachos in my face. I used to get gum in my hair almost every night.

Missy Tip: Peanut butter works for getting gum out of your hair.

I remember one night in El Paso when things almost got out of hand. It was before the main event between John and Scott Casey; the special stipulation was that if John lost, Sunshine would have five minutes alone with me in the ring. It was her big chance to get even for all the times I'd clobbered her with the Gucci purse. But there was like *so* much heat — I mean, as we were walking down the aisle, even before the match started! Fans were jumping up and down, yelling and cursing, tossing Gatorade bottles, half-eaten burritos, even radio batteries.

At that point, the ring was like the safest place. We were too far up the aisle to turn back. I don't know how, but the two cops got us to the ring in one piece, and thank God it was scripted for Scott Casey to win, so Sunshine got her five minutes in the ring with me. We sold it like no one's business that night; I remember, after she had me down, I was whispering to her, "Hit me harder! Harder!" Because I knew that was what the crowd wanted. By the end of the match, it was normal again. The fans had let off their steam. John and I made it back to the dressing room without a problem.

Terry Funk once told me that if I ever got stabbed after a match, I should take it as a compliment; it meant I was doing my job really really well. Maybe. But to be truthful I'm not sure I ever want to do a better job than I did that night in El Paso.

When I first started out in wrestling, I had to put up with a lot of crap. Trying to kill time in the dressing room was the worst. In a lot of the older arenas there was nowhere else to kill time before your match *except* the dressing room. Since the opening matches would already be taking place, wrestlers would always be coming and going, changing into their outfits and then back into their street clothes. John used to set up a chair for me in the corner of the dressing room, facing the wall — like I was the classroom dunce — and then I'd just sit there and read a book. Hey, I read more books in those days than I ever did in high school.

That was when I first started hearing *kayfabe*.

I'd hear it all the time: *Kayfabe* this. *Kayfabe* that. Or just *Kayfabe*!

Well, I had no clue what it meant. I didn't know if it was somebody's girlfriend, or a cuss word, or an inside joke, or what. And it would piss me off; sometimes, I thought the guys were talking about me, like kayfabe was their code name for a woman in the dressing room. So finally I got fed up. I remember, I was facing the wall, and I heard "Kayfabe your trunks." So I turned around, which I never did, and I yelled, "Look, my name's Missy, not Kay!"

That cracked them up so bad!

Later that night, John explained to me about "kayfabe." In the wrestling world, "kayfabe" means like a thousand different things. It's like a secret, all-purpose word. If you hear it by itself, usually, it just means: "Stop talking!" Like if you're gossiping about a wrestler's wife at a bar, and she suddenly walks through the door, whoever spots her first will cut you off with "Kayfabe!"

But it can also be used with other words. "Kayfabe the headlock!" means "Let's finish this up and go on to the next move." Or "Kayfabe the mark!" means "Check out that guy in the front row."

So "Kayfabe your trunks!" had nothing to do with me. It just meant, "You'd better adjust your trunks."

The fact that I was a rookie also meant that I had to drive. I mean, John made me drive *everywhere*. When I was just Melissa, he'd do most of the driving to the matches. But as soon as I became Missy, as soon as I became one of them, it's like *kayfabe* that was the last I saw of the passenger's seat. And when I say, drive, I mean *drive*. I'm talking like four hundred miles to El Paso, then two hundred down to Austin, then another three hundred to Shreveport. And if it was less than two hundred miles, we wouldn't stay overnight; I'd have to drive both ways, back and forth, in one day.

In the beginning I did most of the driving, like four hundred miles at a time

LEARNING THE ROPES

That driver's seat became like a perfect fit for my ass.

All things considered, though, I'd have to say the worst thing about being a rookie was getting ribbed. I think the weirdest rib I got was from Buddy Roberts of the Freebirds. It was in Shreveport, after a match; I had just walked into the bathroom to shower. The second I shut the door, suddenly, I had a feeling I wasn't alone. It wasn't that I heard a noise; it was just that sense you get sometimes after you shut a door. So I started glancing around. I wasn't scared; only the wrestlers had access to the showers, so I kind of guessed it was a rib. I was thinking that somebody was hiding out in one of the stalls, you know, hoping to get a peek.

You expect that sort of thing when you're Missy.

So I figure, *Oh, what the hell? Why not go for it?*

I start to do this slow striptease, unzipping my spandex top just to where my nipples almost show, sliding down my skirt and then slowly wriggling out of it. Then, for my big finish, I kick my left shoe high into the air . . . and then my right. Except the right shoe goes *way* up, higher than I meant, and I hear this soft "Owww." So I glance up, and there's Buddy Roberts. He's hunched up against the ceiling, straddling the top edge of a mirror and a shower nozzle. And his fly is unzipped.

He's about to pee on me.

So I go running out of that bathroom with my boobs flying out of my top and my panties riding up my butt, half screaming and half cursing, and the rest of the wrestlers — including John! — are just rolling on the floor hysterical.

After I calm down, John tells me that the Freebirds always pee on people they like. It's like a privilege to get peed on by a Freebird.

It's like a ritual, a sign of respect.

Well, thanks. But no thank you.

Lots of wrestlers, even nowadays, don't like valets. It's nothing personal, usually. They just don't like the *idea* of stuff going on outside the ring; they think it's, you know, a distraction, like it takes away from the athletic performance of the wrestlers. Hey, even some fans feel that way. They look at valets as cheap gimmicks to help build up wrestlers who can't get over on their own.

So let's set the record straight.

It's a fact of life in wrestling that not everyone who works well in the ring also talks well. Dean Malenko is like that. People in the business used to say that Dean Malenko could wrestle a broomstick and make it look like a good match. He could outwork Hulk Hogan, The Rock, Steve Austin, the Macho Man. You name him, Dean Malenko could outwork him. But he never got over like the big names because he couldn't talk. Another example is a tag team like the Midnight Express — Sweet Stan Lane and Bobby Eaton. Back in the mid-1980's, the Midnight Express were two of the best workers in the business. I mean, they could flat out wrestle. Belly-to-back suplexes, roll-over pin combinations, moonsaults off the top rope — there was nothing they couldn't do, and whatever they were doing, they sold it. You'd hear (or at least you'd *think* you heard) their dropkicks hitting the sides of their opponents' heads. These guys could go forty-five minutes in the ring and never repeat a move. The problem was they couldn't put themselves over. You'd stick them in front of the camera for an interview after a match, and it was like, "Yeah, we're going to kick the Freebirds butts. We're going to kick their butts . . . so bad! They won't know what hit 'em, that's how bad we're going to kick their butts. In Tulsa . . . on Friday night . . . in the Civic Center. Be there!"

So the Midnight Express hooked up with Jim Cornett, who's a manager — and who's just about the best talker in the business. Wow, could that guy talk! He could talk the ear off a brass donkey. Plus, he had that high, squeaky voice; even if you didn't want to listen to him, he got over. He'd stand up in front of the camera, in between Stan and Bobby, and he'd get a cue, and then he was off. It would be like, "Freebirds, you better be going to church between now and next Friday night in the Tulsa Civic Center. 'Cause the Midnight Express is going to kill you. They're going to tear you into itsy bitsy pieces, and then they're going to collect up the itsy bitsy pieces, sew them back together, then tear you up again. I'm warning you, it's not going to be a pretty thing to watch. You folks out in Tulsa, if you've got weak stomachs, you better stay home. Or if you show up, you better bring Milk of Magnesia. Because it's going to turn your stomach, what the Midnight Express is going to do to the Freebirds. . . ."

I mean, Jim Cornett could go on like that for an hour if he didn't get the signal to cut.

But the drawback with male managers is, yes, they put their wrestlers over, but they don't always put people in the seats. They weren't the focus of many storylines; they didn't develop angles on their own. In other words, the action was still inside the ring.

That began to change with Sunshine.

First of all, she was a woman, and she was kind of sexy, so she brought in fans who would otherwise never have come to watch two large guys grunting and sweating inside the ring. It's like, suddenly, there was eye-candy outside the ring while the match was going on. Then came the Sunshine-Precious feud — which was an angle that started outside the ring and ended up in a catfight inside the ring. But Jimmy Garvin, who brought them both into the business, was a good talker, so he didn't need Sunshine or Precious to say very much during his interviews. They just kind of smiled and nodded their heads.

That's when I arrived on the scene. All I did was take the valet role to the next logical level. Since John was such a bad talker, I became a combination valet and manager. I wore low cut blouses and hot pants to the ring, which brought in the horny guys, but I also had to develop my own persona since I was the one hyping matches during our interviews.

Before long, the bookers figured out another benefit to working storylines around valets. It gave them more flexibility. They could keep feuds going longer since the valets made the outcomes of main events less predictable. I mean, in the past you knew what was going to happen just by listening to the interviews. The babyface would come on, and he'd be all modest, looking determined, but speaking in a soft voice; whereas the heel would be arrogant, pounding on his chest, shouting straight into the camera. Yet they were both saying pretty much the same thing. "We're going to settle this thing once and for all next Saturday in Lubbock."

Blah, blah, blah.

The trouble was that next Saturday, in Lubbock, it had to end. No matter how well the two guys worked together, there was nowhere else to go with the storyline. The babyface pinned the heel. The rule used to be that the heel never won at the house shows. Good had to triumph over Evil, so the paying customers would go home happy. Then, afterwards, the babyface got paired up with a different heel, and the heel got paired up with a different babyface, and the entire cycle would start up again.

But if a heel had a valet, well, that meant the heel could win . . . *with the valet's interference.* That way, it wasn't like Evil was triumphing over

Workin' the Missy angle at Le Bar Bat

Good; it was more like Good was about to triumph over Evil, but then at the last second Good got sucker-punched by Evil's valet. (Kind of like the Garden of Eden!) Plus, the babyface could never retaliate. Not against a woman. That was another advantage valets had over male managers. Whereas a babyface could piledrive a Jimmy Hart or a Jim Cornett in the middle of the ring, he could never lay a finger on a valet — even if she was a heel. All he could do was shake his fist and warn her not to get involved next time. Which of course never worked. Eventually, he had to find his own valet to fight for him.

Meanwhile, the feud kept going . . . and people kept paying money to fill those seats . . . and, best of all, Missy kept getting those lovely checks to take to the bank.

The first paycheck I ever got from the Von Erichs was for fifty dollars. I know, you're thinking, *Fifty dollars! Big whoop!* But I still have the stub from that check. It seemed unreal. I mean, all I'd done was run down the aisle to the ring, clobber Sunshine with my Gucci purse, and collect fifty bucks.

Five minutes work!

But in the beginning that's how it was. On a good night at the Sportatorium, not even a sell out, I'd take home about $200. And it was never more than five or ten minutes work. And when I say work, I mean it was like being paid for nothing. I would just stand at ringside and go into my act. But every so often, Sunshine and I would get into a little brawl — she'd chase me around the ring a couple of times (she was the babyface, and I was the heel, so I had to be the chicken), and finally I'd climb into the ring, and then she'd have me cornered. Then we'd grab hair, tie up and tumble around. She's the one who taught me how to do that, how to grab hair and roll without getting hurt. (You grab deep into the hair and hold on tight; if you grab the loose ends, you'll pull the hair out.) Since she had seniority, she would always call our fights; it was like dancing, and she would always lead. For instance, she'd whisper "Come with me." Then she'd reach for my hair and drag me around the ring; I would just follow her. You've got to talk, or else someone might get hurt. She'd say, "Now I'm going to choke you" or "Now get me down" or "Roll over, two times, now." Or, sometimes, she would just say "Sell this!" — you know, like go for a big reaction.

Whoever's calling the match also has to watch for the cue to end. All the preliminary matches, from the first to the last, have to end on time. Or else the main event winds up cut short. So Sunshine would pick up the cue, usually from the ring announcer, to wind up our catfight, and then she'd whisper to me, "All right, let's go home."

Going home, in wrestling, means ending the match.

The first catfight we had, though, I started to crack up in the middle of it. She was calling the match, real serious, and she had this look on her face like she wanted to kill me, and meanwhile, she's whispering instructions. It just cracked me up. Luckily, my hair was long, so it was covering my face. But I was cracking up, and she was whispering to me, "Don't laugh, damn it! Don't laugh!" Afterwards, she was balling me out in the dressing room, "Don't ever laugh! If you laugh again, I'll really pull your hair out!" But then she started to crack up; I mean, the entire thing was so silly, she couldn't even keep a straight face balling me out.

The two of us bonded real quick, me and Sunshine. She had nowhere to dress either, so whenever we were working a show, we guarded the bathroom door for each other. Naturally, she'd gotten all the ribs I got — only worse, because she came first. I think the Freebirds actually did pee on her.

Sunshine and I played that catfight routine out maybe a hundred times. The biggest payday I had with WCCW was for a February show in Fort Worth. I showed up ringside in a blue dress, and we gimmicked it that she snuck up behind me and yanked it off; I ended up running back up the aisle in a one-piece teddy and hose. We both got $1200 for five minutes work. Not bad, huh?

The feud between me and Sunshine came to a head in Dallas at Texas Stadium. In a mud match. It was the main event — actually, it *had* to be the main event since the ring was going to be covered with mud afterwards.

It was the blow off, you know, the end of the angle, so we had to build up to it gradually. For months in advance, I was getting the better of her during the TV tapings. (Remember, the catfights were *only* for the house shows.) As far as the television audience knew, she could never quite get her hands on me; she'd chase me around the ring, lunge at me and just miss — and then Scott Casey or John or even the ring announcers would hold her back. I mean, week after week, I kept getting away. I'd pull out a chair from underneath her, or I'd yank her hair from behind, and then I'd run back to the dressing room. One time, I knocked her out with the Gucci purse . . . and then spray-painted her yellow.

Naturally, it couldn't go on forever. So Ken Mantel, the booker, came up with the idea of a mud match to end the storyline. The way we introduced it was I came out one week while she was doing an interview, and behind my back, I was carrying a mud pie. The camera got a shot of it,

LEARNING THE ROPES

and the entire audience saw me walking up to her with it, but she was just glaring at me. Then, suddenly, I smashed the mud pie into her face. So she's standing there, in the interview area, with mud dripping down her face, and she looks into the camera and says, "All right, Missy. You like mud so much? Then it's me and you, next week, in the mud. We're going to get down and dirty in Texas Stadium. I'm going to mess you up, tramp!"

The night before the mud match, I was scared to death. I kept waking up in the middle of the night, gasping for air, kicking John and waking him up. Then he'd hold me tight till I fell back asleep.

The next day, I was hyperventilating so bad John broke down and drove the entire way to the stadium. I guess that meant I wasn't a rookie anymore. But I had my head between my knees most of the trip.

The thing of it was, I was just getting used to being in front of crowds. I was just getting comfortable. But I'd never done a show like this. Just the number of cars in the stadium parking lot shook me up. The first pop from crowd, while I was still in the dressing room, scared the bejeezes out of me. Sunshine and I peeked out from underneath the stands. I mean, Texas Stadium was *packed*; I think there were sixty thousand people. Plus, like I said, the mud match was the main event, so the two of us had to wait out the entire show backstage. I think I must have gone to the bathroom ten times, and Sunshine, who was usually pretty calm, was trembling. I mean, I could see her trembling. Meanwhile, wrestlers were coming back to the dressing room after their matches, and they're all psyched and whooping it up and full of adrenaline from the noise of the crowd.

The second I walked through the tunnel under the stands and out into the stadium, flashbulbs started going off. It was blinding. Then it felt like about a mile walk from the tunnel to the ring in the center of the ball field. I was wearing a one piece bathing suit, low cut but pretty conservative, but I swear in front of all those people, with the roar of the crowd and the flashes of light, at that moment, I felt totally naked. Then when I finally climbed into the ring, there was just a baby pool in the middle of it with maybe six inches of mud. I remember thinking how surreal it was, how sixty thousand people were standing and screaming for something that was about to happen in a baby pool in six inches of mud.

I'd guess we were actually in the mud for about five minutes — you know, there's only so much rolling around in the mud you can do. But there was like a big drama we planned out beforehand. First Sunshine stepped into the mud. Then I grabbed the mike from the ring announcer and said, "No way, no way, I'm not getting in that mud!" And Sunshine, meanwhile, was just standing with her hands on her hips, waiting for me to climb in. It was like a standoff. Every time she'd make a move across the mud towards me, I'd jump backwards away from the baby pool. Then finally I said, "I'm not going to do this. I don't have to do this. It's not in my contract."

That's when Ken Mantel came running out from the tunnel, waving a sheet of paper. Then he climbed into the ring and grabbed the mike and said, "Missy Hyatt, this is your contract. Do you see that signature at the bottom."

I nodded that I did.

"That's your signature Missy Hyatt. You have to do this."

The crowd roared; I mean, it was deafening.

So I grabbed the mike back and yelled at them, "Shut up! Shut up! I'm not going to do it. I don't care what the stupid contract says!"

Then the crowd started to boo.

"Shut up!" I yelled at them. "Shut up!"

Just then, as I was telling the crowd to shut up, Sunshine ran across the mud pit, caught me by the hair and yanked me into backwards into the mud. The crowd just erupted; it sounded like a jet engine revving up.

Once the two of us were in the mud, it was actually kind of fun. I mean, if you've never done it, it sounds kind of gross. But I had a good time. We were like a couple of pigs in slop; we were rolling around, flinging mud in each other's faces. Finally, after the five minutes were up, Sunshine rolled on top of me and pinned my shoulders. Then the referee, Dave Manning, who was circling the baby pool on the outside, jumped into position, and he counted me out, "One, two, three."

The crowd went wild again.

Afterwards, when Dave Manning was raising up Sunshine's hand, she and I kind of made eye contact. We grabbed him and threw him backwards into the mud. It was the only ad lib the entire night.

The last memory I have of that show was in the shower. Sunshine and

I are showering at the same time, and there's mud everywhere — a trail of it from the dressing room to the showers. It's a Saturday night, and the Dallas Cowboys are scheduled to play a home game the next day. We both start glancing around; I mean, it's an unbelievable mess.

Then I start laughing. "I sure hope someone's going to clean this up before tomorrow. Or else Coach Landry is going to be pissed."

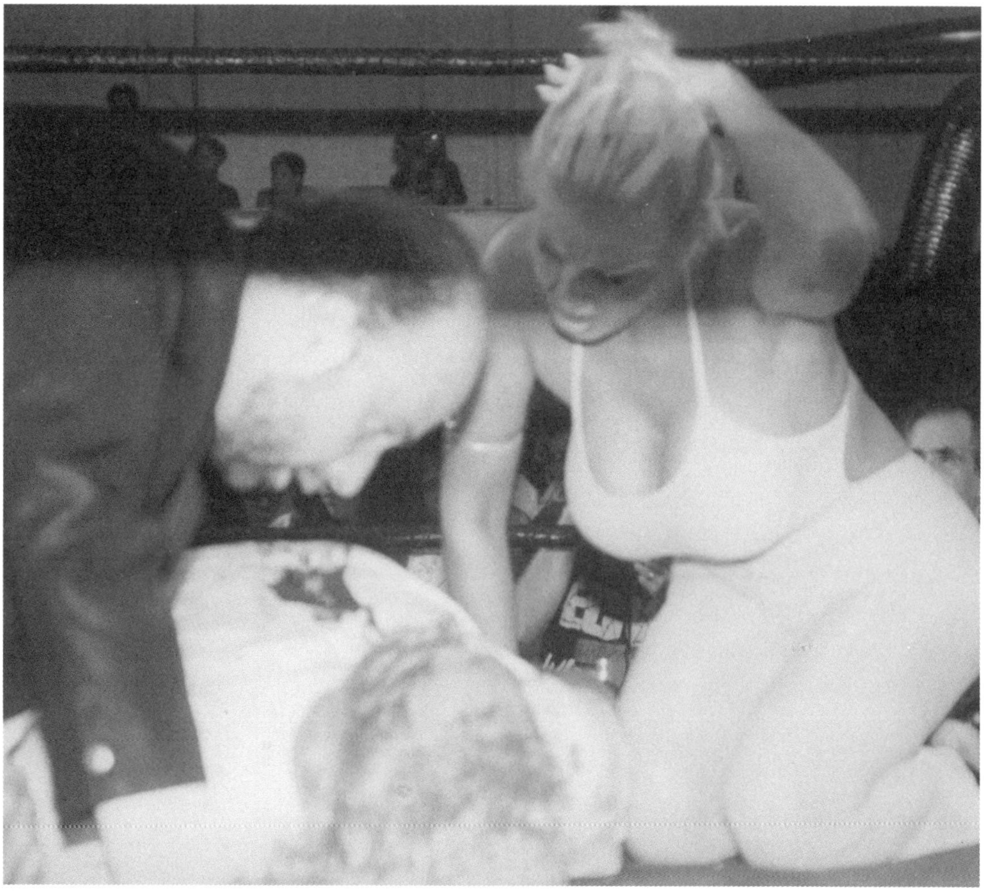

3

Living on Tulsa Time

Oklahoma, UWF

John and I would have stayed with WCCW a lot longer if Fritz's booker, Ken Mantel, hadn't jumped to the Universal Wrestling Federation in 1986. We had even cooked up a new angle; I was going to turn on John and go with Gino Hernandez — which would start a feud between the two of them. But then Ken got the call from Cowboy Bill Watts to come to Tulsa. I felt awful about leaving Fritz after he'd given me my first break in the business, but Ken was the one who gave John a big push in the organization, the one who always booked us in semi-mains and main events; I mean, he really looked after us. So John and I followed him to the UWF. He took the two of us and the Freebirds.

The UWF circuit covered more territory than WCCW — which operated out of Texas and Louisiana. The UWF held shows in Oklahoma, Arkansas, Tennessee, Mississippi . . . plus Texas and Louisiana. So it was too far between arenas to drive. That meant we'd have to travel by plane, at least part of the time. If for no other reason than that, it felt like a step up.

Another step up was the kind of contracts we signed. Instead of getting paid on the house, like with WCCW, Bill Watts signed John and me to one year deals for $50,000. That was it, period. Didn't matter if twenty-five people showed up for our matches or if twenty-five thousand showed up. It was a regular paycheck. Like in the real world.

Now the UWF had just one girl at the time, Dark Journey. She was managing a wrestler called Missing Link who had this wild hair, like Buckwheat from the Little Rascals, and who painted his face green. So that was the feud that was scripted — me and John against Dark Journey and Missing Link.

The way we were introduced to the UWF fans was through Jack Victory, a wrestler who John had tag-teamed with a few times in WCCW. Jack had come to the UWF a couple of months earlier and was feuding with Missing Link, and Dark Journey kept interfering in their matches, helping Link win — and each time she did, the crowd ate it up, since she and Link were the babyfaces and Jack was the heel. But then Jack starts doing promos, saying, "You better watch out, Dark Journey. I'm calling in my friends to take care of you."

That goes on for maybe a couple of weeks, just long enough for the announcers to coax information out of him, but Jack always cuts the interviews short and walks off camera with this kind of *Just you wait and see!* smile on his face. Then, finally, during a TV taping, he struts out to the middle of the ring unannounced; he's not even scheduled to wrestle, but he takes the microphone and starts to talk. Naturally, the crowd boos him like crazy. But he just stands there, grinning, waiting for the fans to quiet down. "Like I was saying," he says, "I'd like to introduce a couple of friends of mine from Texas. . . ."

Which cues our music.

A second later, John and I walk through the curtains, strut down the aisle and climb into the ring.

Meanwhile, the announcers, Jim Ross and Michael Hayes, are yelling, "Oh my God! It's Hollywood John Tatum and Missy Hyatt. They're here in the UWF, and you can bet they're going to be kicking butt and taking names."

That was the beginning of the feud.

Dark Journey was a damn pretty girl — I'll give her that. Her mother was black and her father was white, and she wound up with real exotic facial features. All right, maybe she was more than just pretty. She was kind of beautiful. I'd heard rumors before I got to Tulsa that she was a cokehead, but I didn't pay too much attention to them; I'm sure she'd heard all sorts of rumors about me. That's how the wrestling world works.

What I *did* know about her, what I knew *for sure* I mean, was that she was in the middle of a major blow-up in the locker room two weeks before John and I arrived. The thing was, she got her break in the business because she was dating Dick Slater — who was one of the big stars in the UWF. He brought her in as a valet; after the success WCCW had with valets, all the organizations were suddenly on the lookout for pretty girls. Except she had no experience — unless blowing Dick Slater counts as experience. Plus, until I showed up, there was no other girl to work an angle with her.

By the time John and I arrived, Dick Slater was out of the picture, too. Now here's the dirt.

Two weeks before Ken brought in John and me from WCCW, Dark Journey had left Dick Slater — who was like old enough to be her father — and shacked up for a weekend in the apartment of a young wrestler named Steve Borden.

That's Sting to you.

Naturally, Slater found out about it, probably from Dark Journey herself, and naturally he flipped out. The next week, he came storming into the dressing room looking for Sting, and he found him in the bathroom putting on his face paint. Slater beat the living crap out of him. Sting didn't even put up a fight. He just let himself get beat up: first, because he knew he'd been caught, and second, because he was just starting out in the business and Slater had a lot of buddies who could have screwed with his career. Sting never talked about what happened, not to me, but I heard from a couple of wrestlers who were in the dressing room that night that he came staggering out of the bathroom with his eyes swollen shut and his mouth all busted up and his cheekbones bruised. The worst of it was that afterwards he had to go back into the bathroom, put on his makeup over the cuts and bruises, and head out to the ring and wrestle.

Slater left the UWF the next week.

🍸

Working with Dark Journey was a nightmare from the very start. I mean, I guess I was little spoiled from my experience with Sunshine — who always worked light and easy. But Dark Journey was the *worst*. She beat my ass every night. It didn't matter how much we rehearsed our moves ahead of time. She would chase me around the ring, just like we rehearsed it, and she would grab me by the hair, just like we rehearsed it — and then she'd get a pop from the crowd, and she'd just snap. The adrenaline would get to her. She'd hear the crowd roar, and then, suddenly, it was like she went into vapor lock.

That happens to lots of wrestlers, actually. The pop from the crowd gets to them. I've felt it myself — especially being a heel. The crowd reacts to something you do, like a slap or a kick, and it's as if the noise lifts you out of your body. It feels like you're floating on the wave of noise. It's the best high, better than any drug. But it's dangerous if you keep floating — which is what happens a lot with rookies. They'll clamp a sleeper on their opponent, get that pop from the crowd, that adrenaline rush, and then the forearm tightens across the throat, and a second later the other guy's gasping for air. It's called *shooting*. That's when you apply a hold for real. Certain guys are notorious for doing it, sometimes on purpose. The Road Warriors are like that. Taz was like that, especially when he was with ECW. He'd be in the middle of a match, and then, for no reason, he'd start to shoot. No one knew if he was doing it on purpose or if he was just reacting to the crowd. But I know more than one wrestler in ECW who wouldn't step into the ring with Taz.

Most of the time, though, it's an accident. You start shooting your opponent, you catch yourself, and then you apologize for it in the dressing room. But Dark Journey was shooting on me like every night. She would be pounding my head into the mat, and as the crowd got louder and louder, I could feel her banging my head harder and harder. And I'd be yelling, "Ow! . . . Ow . . . OW!" Or even "Stop it! . . . *Stop it! STOP IT!*" But nothing got through to her. Her eyes would go glassy, and at that point, it was like a real fight, and I was trying to kick her off me.

Then, afterwards, I'd wind up hobbling back up the aisle to the dressing room. The fans along the aisle always thought it was part of the show, and they'd be like, *Oh, poor Missy!* You know, sarcastic. But then, a minute later, I'd start screaming, "That girl is freaking crazy!" But the guys in the dressing room would just laugh. They figured it was a chick thing.

I mean, I only worked with her for like six months. But the bitch broke my thumb, chipped two of my teeth and yanked out so much of my hair, I had a bald spot.

Like I said, I'd heard rumors that she was a cokehead.

It's not like I never tried to talk to her about it. But she was just so dumb. She couldn't do an interview to save her life, couldn't remember the dates or the arena names. What's the saying? Dumb as an oyster fart. That was her. For instance, we had one routine that we did two weeks in a row — maybe twelve different cities, but the identical match. Missing Link would get on top of John for a pin, and I'd stop the count by yanking his leg from outside the ring. Then Dark Journey was supposed to chase me around two ring posts, and I would jump through the ropes and into the ring, and she would jump in after me, and we'd come together for a second and roll, and then John would grab me out. I mean, how hard is that? But we did it two weeks straight, and she screwed it up every time. The first week she caught me outside the ring. The second week she forgot to jump in after me and just kept running. The third week she wouldn't let go of my hair when John tried to grab me out. She had absolutely no clue.

Like I said, the UWF covered much more territory than WCCW did — which meant that the venues ranged from nice modern arenas to rat holes. And when I say rat holes, I mean houses where even the rats were dragging their asses around, as if they were thinking, *Please, God, get me out of here!*

I remember this one place north of New Orleans called the Le Range Civic Center. John and I couldn't find it at first, so we had to stop the car and ask the way. We pulled up at a two pump gas station, like Goober's garage, and (I kid you not!) the guy starts giving us directions like, "Well, you keep going down this road for about another mile, and then you take a left at the big metal chicken, and then a right at the broken fence post. . . ."

So we finally find the place, and it turns out to be a rodeo arena. Cow smell. Dirt floors. Stalls to the left and right. We walk inside, and at the end of a long corridor, we come to two doors. On the left door, there's a magic marker sign that reads GOOD GUYS. On the right door, there's a sign that reads BAD GUYS. John and I walk though the BAD GUYS door, and it's just one big room, maybe fifty feet by fifty feet, with a cracked toilet right in the center.

I turned to John and said, "Remind me to cut my throat."

He just kind of shrugged. "Hey, babe, it's the business."

He took it a little more personally, though, when he found out the Civic Center was running a bake sale that night . . . and cakes were being auctioned off between matches.

🍸

Lots of wrestlers who were working with the UWF around that time went on to become major stars. There was Sting, Terry Taylor, Rick Steiner, Jack Victory, Hacksaw Jim Duggan, Steve Williams (a.k.a. Dr. Death), Ted DiBiase (a.k.a. The Million Dollar Man). The Freebirds were already big when they came over from WCCW with me and John, but they got even bigger. It's no coincidence that all their careers took off after wrestling with the UWF because Bill Watts had two of the best bookers in the business. One was Ken Mantel.

The other was Hot Stuff Eddie Gilbert.

The strange thing was, Eddie wasn't even an official booker. He was under contract to manage Sting and Rick Steiner, and he also wrestled himself occasionally. As a matter of fact, lots of people said that if Eddie were two inches taller, he had the talent to be a world champion. Not just for an indie either; I mean, it's easy enough to be somebody's world champ if you're willing to wrestle in a Beaver Lodge. Eddie had the goods to be a world champion for WWF or WCW. He was a great worker, and he was one of the best talkers in the business. But he just didn't look like a world champion; he didn't have the height, you know, like Hulk Hogan or Lex Luger or Sting. Eddie was only five foot ten. It's all about perception.

But Eddie was smart enough to play the cards he'd been dealt. Even though he was only a couple of years older than I was, he'd been around the business long enough to realize that his future was scripting storylines and matches. He came from a wrestling family. His father, Tommy Gilbert, was a well-known wrestler who later became a referee. His grandfather used to wrestle in traveling carnivals in the 1930's and 40's. So it was in his genes. His mother told me that when Eddie was eleven years old, watching wrestling on TV in Memphis, he was already booking shows. You know, he'd write down the matches he thought would work, the feuds he thought should be developed, the angles, the blow offs. He scripted entire storylines. He used real wrestlers if he could, but when there was no

Terry Taylor and Eddie Gilbert

wrestler around who suited the angle he wanted to work, he'd make up his own fictitious wrestlers. His mom saved his old booking sheets.

So Eddie was like Ken Mantel's unofficial assistant booker. He didn't even get paid for doing it. But I'd say about half the storylines in the UWF were Eddie's ideas.

And, yes, Eddie's the one who came up with the idea of Hot Stuff and Hyatt International. It was right after the feud with Dark Journey and Missing Link wound down, so John and I were kind of floating. Eddie came up with the concept of an alliance between his tag team — Sting and Steiner — and my tag team — John Tatum and Jack Victory. He picked up on the "Hyatt" name and made it into like a corporate merger.

Naturally, that meant Eddie and I would have to spend a lot of time together. Now you could be cynical and think that's the reason he came up with the angle in the first place. But the truth is, Eddie was never like that. To begin with, he had just gotten married a couple of months earlier to a girl named Teri. Plus, he knew I was with John, and he liked John. Plus, it wasn't like there were sparks flying between us the first time we met. It was just a handshake; I don't even remember it, to be honest. But once the storyline got going, once we were working as Hot Stuff and Hyatt, we became friends. He subscribed to *The Wrestling Observer* — which is like the *National Enquirer* of pro wrestling — and the two of us would sit around before matches and read it from cover to cover. I think that was when I first felt it. You know, the tingle. The chemistry. Like, we'd be ringside during tag team matches, and our eyes would meet, and then we'd both glance down real quick and pretend nothing had happened. That kind of stuff. After a while, he'd start telling me how he'd gotten married for all the wrong reasons, how his wife had lied to him about being pregnant. But neither of us wanted to make the first move.

Meanwhile, John and I were fighting all the time. We'd been together for just over two years, and when I say "together," I mean *together*. Not just at work, not just at home, but we'd be on the road for five hours at a stretch, just the two of us in the front seat of a car with nothing to do but argue over radio stations. I mean, it got to the point where he'd have a golf game scheduled for six o'clock Saturday morning, and I'd wake up as soon as I heard the door shut behind him. Then I'd just sit in the kitchen with a cup of coffee and listen to the sound of him not being there.

What complicated things even more was when the announcers began to pick up on it — you know, the sexual tension between me and Eddie. I'm sure they thought they were ad libbing, but they started firing questions at us during interviews like, "So, is it strictly business between the two of you?"

Then Eddie would answer, "Yes, it's strictly business."

And I'd be, "That's right. *Strictly* business."

But it's not the kind of situation you can hide. Not when the truth was written all over our faces. I think it even came across on television.

LIVING ON TULSA TIME

The shit hit the fan in Dallas.

It was nothing Eddie and I arranged in advance; it wasn't a special day; it was just the day when the predicament became unbearable. I phoned Eddie the second John stepped out of the house; he answered on the first ring, and as soon as I heard his voice, I just said, "Meet me at the Holiday Inn." Then I hung up the phone. I didn't even wait for him to say, "All right, I'll be there." I just hung up and rushed out the door.

I didn't come home until the next morning — to pack my bags and move out. By that afternoon, I'd found an apartment in Baton Rouge. By that night, I was living on my own in Louisiana.

Strictly business!

When I walked into Ken Mantel's office, the day after I moved out, and told him that I wanted him to split up me and John as soon as he could, he said no.

"Look," I said, "I don't want to work with him anymore."

He told me that Hot Stuff and Hyatt International was too good an angle to break up, and that I worked better with John. Besides, Eddie was more a manager than a wrestler at that point, so Ken thought it would look strange to have two managers for one tag team, Sting and Steiner. I pleaded and pleaded, but in the end, Ken shook his head no and told me that I would have to be professional about it.

That meant that Eddie and I would have to sneak around. Not for John's sake. For the fans' sake. I mean, Bill Watts threatened to fire both of us if the fans found out what was happening. So Eddie and I couldn't take the same flights to shows. We couldn't socialize after the matches. If we rode together to a local show, I would have to duck down in the back seat when we got near the arena. It was torture.

I remember one time I wanted to cook dinner for Eddie at my new apartment in Baton Rouge. The problem was that there were lots of wrestling fans living on my block and even in my building. The entire neighborhood was crawling with them; I used to be recognized on the street like ten times a day. They'd be like, "Hey, Missy, what's going on? How's John doing? You guys have got a tough match coming up, huh?"

And I'd just smile and nod.

But this one time I was determined to cook Eddie a chicken dinner. Except I'm not a good cook, so I was on the phone with my mom the entire afternoon saying, "Yeah, the chicken's in the pot. What do I do now?" Meanwhile, Eddie's got to put on a wig and hat so no one recognizes him when he comes up to the front door.

So I let him in, and we start to smooch for a couple of minutes, and then, when I turn around, there's smoke coming from the kitchen. So we rush to the stove, and the chicken's on fire, and at first we're throwing glasses of water at the pot, but the flames keep getting higher and higher, and then Eddie starts yelling, "Pour salt on it! Pour salt on it!" So I'm like lunging at the fire with this teensy-weensy salt shaker, and the flames are singeing the hair on my arm.

Finally, Eddie remembers there's a fire extinguisher in the hall, just outside the front door, so he runs out and snatches it, and then he sprays foam all over the chicken and puts out the fire.

Except now there's smoke billowing out the door of the apartment, out the windows, everywhere, and fire alarms are going off left and right. Five minutes later, two fire trucks are rolling up in front of the building. By now, neighbors are crowding around the front door, peeking in to find out if I'm all right. So the firemen arrive, look around, then kind of laugh about the ruined chicken. Then they leave, and I shut the front door.

Eddie was hiding in the closet, inhaling smoke, the entire time.

Meanwhile, John was being mean to me every chance he had. Again, I went to Ken's office. "I can't work with him anymore. I tried, Ken, but I just can't. He's being so mean to me. I am not walking out to the ring with him ever again. I'd rather quit. I *will* quit."

I guess that got to him.

But he still didn't want to drop the Hot Stuff and Hyatt International storyline. Not all of a sudden, without explanation. So he said like, *Okay, okay, we'll break you up* — except he decided he would work the in breakup as a new angle. That's the way it is in wrestling. Nothing's thrown out. Today's trash is tomorrow's sit-down dinner.

So for the next month, the angle became: *What's wrong with Hot Stuff and Hyatt International?* The announcers were cued in on it, and whenever we'd come to the ring, they'd be saying stuff like, "It's been very obvious for weeks now that Missy Hyatt's world is coming apart at the seams. The only question is can the corporation survive?"

Meanwhile, I would be thinking, *Stop the presses! Reality comes to wrestling!*

The deal we worked out with Ken Mantel was for Eddie to woo me away from John gradually, not suddenly. So the next week on TV, I'm ringside for John and Jack's match, and Eddie comes out from the dressing room with a bouquet of roses. And I'm like, "Oh, thank you very much!" — you know, all blushing and smiling. Then John catches sight of what's going on, and he jumps out of the ring, throws the roses on the ground and chases Eddie away. But then the following week, Eddie shows up with

Pillman Show, with D'Lo Brown

a box of chocolates. And again John chases him away. Then after that it's a bottle of Chanel perfume. Week after week, we played that same routine over and over.

The entire time, I don't think John and I said a civil word to one another. It was horrible. He still had some of my stuff at his place, mostly clothes and silverware, stuff like that — oh, and a sun bed. But he changed the lock on the door and wouldn't let me back into the apartment to get it.

I mean, I can't wait for the blow off in the ring.

The break finally comes during a tag team match. John and Jack squash a couple of jobbers, and then I jump into the ring to raise their hands . . . and then, suddenly, Eddie runs out to the ring to confront John. Except just as John's about to clobber him, Sting and Steiner rush out. Jack runs from the ring, all scared, and Sting and Steiner tackle John to the canvas. They start pummeling him, and Eddie's getting in kicks, and the crowd's booing their heads off. Hey, we're practically making John into an instant babyface! Then the three of them hold up John, twist his arms behind his back, and they call me into the ring. And Eddie's screaming, "Hit him, Missy! Hit him!"

I hesitate for a split second, but then I haul off and nail him in the face with the Gucci purse. He drops to the canvas and juices, and now he's bleeding all over the place. I mean, it was one of the all time juices; he was gushing like a stuck pig. Really, he made my Gucci purse into a legend. The TV audience must have been thinking, *What in hell does that girl have in that bag?* I gave John one last kick in the back, and then I left the ring arm in arm with Eddie.

On the way back to the dressing room, I remember thinking, "Son of a bitch got his blood on my Gucci purse!"

Even now, I get asked more often about juicing than any other *how'd-they-do-that?* wrestling question. "Juicing" is like the dumbest thing in the world. The wrestler actually takes a razor blade and cuts his own forehead. I'm not joking — I wish I was.

That's actually the safe way to do it. But there's also juicing "the hard way." That's when you have a pre-existing cut on your forehead, and before a match you swallow a lot of aspirins to thin your blood. The skin on your forehead is so weak anyway that a couple of shots with a knuckle will open you right up. That way is more dangerous, though, because you never know how deep a cut you're going to open. Eddie hard-wayed one time and bled on and off for two days. Last year, Diamond Dallas Paige cut himself for the Brian Pillman Memorial Show, and afterwards I saw him backstage — I mean, the poor guy must have hit an artery — and I was like, "Dallas, *dude!*"

I heard Paige actually wound up going to a plastic surgeon that night.

Looking back at the soap opera angle Ken Mantel forced on the three of us, John, Eddie and me, I realize now that that was a turning point not just in the lives of the three of us; it became a kind of turning point for professional wrestling. The breakup of Hot Stuff and Hyatt International went on for *so* long, and it got *so* much ink in the wrestling mags, that every booker in every two-bit organization noticed it. It was a like new way to fill up television time.

In fact, you could argue that that was the moment in the evolution of wrestling when the focus began to shift. What was going on outside the ring suddenly became as interesting as what was going on inside the ring. I mean, inside the ring you were pretty limited; you basically had two guys, or four guys, or six guys . . . or midgets . . . or women, beating the crap out of each other. You had violence, period.

But outside the ring . . . you had *sex*.

It was like a lightbulb switching on above the head of every local booker in America.

If I was a major heel before, when I was with John, well, I was *the* heel after I went with Eddie. The two of us were the most hated couple in the UWF, probably in all of wrestling. Bill Watts had to hire extra security for our matches. It wasn't just spitting and throwing gum as I was walking towards the ring. One night, at the Memphis Coliseum, the fans started flinging Gatorade bottles from the mezzanine. And I don't mean empty bottles! People were buying full bottles just to fling them at me. They were hitting the floor all around me and exploding, splashing me and soaking the fans who were sitting ringside. Just as the announcement came that the show would be canceled if they didn't stop, one last bottle came down and it me in the left leg. I was bleeding as I limped back to the dressing room.

The crowd was cheering as they watched me.

Another time, in Columbus, Georgia, a lady grabbed me by the hair as I was walking towards the ring. I mean, she *really* got hold of me; I couldn't pull myself free. When security finally got her off me, they patted her down and found a butcher knife in her jacket pocket. It shook me up pretty bad, but it also reminded me of what Terry Funk told me: "If you ever get stabbed after a match, that means you did your job really really well."

Well, baby, I almost got stabbed on my way *to* the ring, before the match. So what did that mean?

I remember one of the proudest moments of my career happened in a doctor's office in Georgia — I think it was in 1991. There were only two people in the waiting room, me and a young guy. After about ten minutes, he walked up to me and said, "You're Missy Hyatt, aren't you?"

"Yeah."

"Damn, I hate your guts when I see you on the TV"

"Really?" I said. "But you keep watching, don't you?"

"Yeah."

Then he asked for my autograph.

My mom used to worry about it though. She'd watch me on television and read about me in the magazines, and like once a week I'd get a phone call from her asking, "Why can't you be nice?"

"That's not my job, Mom."

"But you *are* nice."

Then I'm like, "Not so loud! Not so loud!"

Actually, at that point, neither of my parents talked much to their friends about what I was doing. That changed later on, when I was on TBS, but back then it was difficult for my folks to understand why I was doing what I was doing.

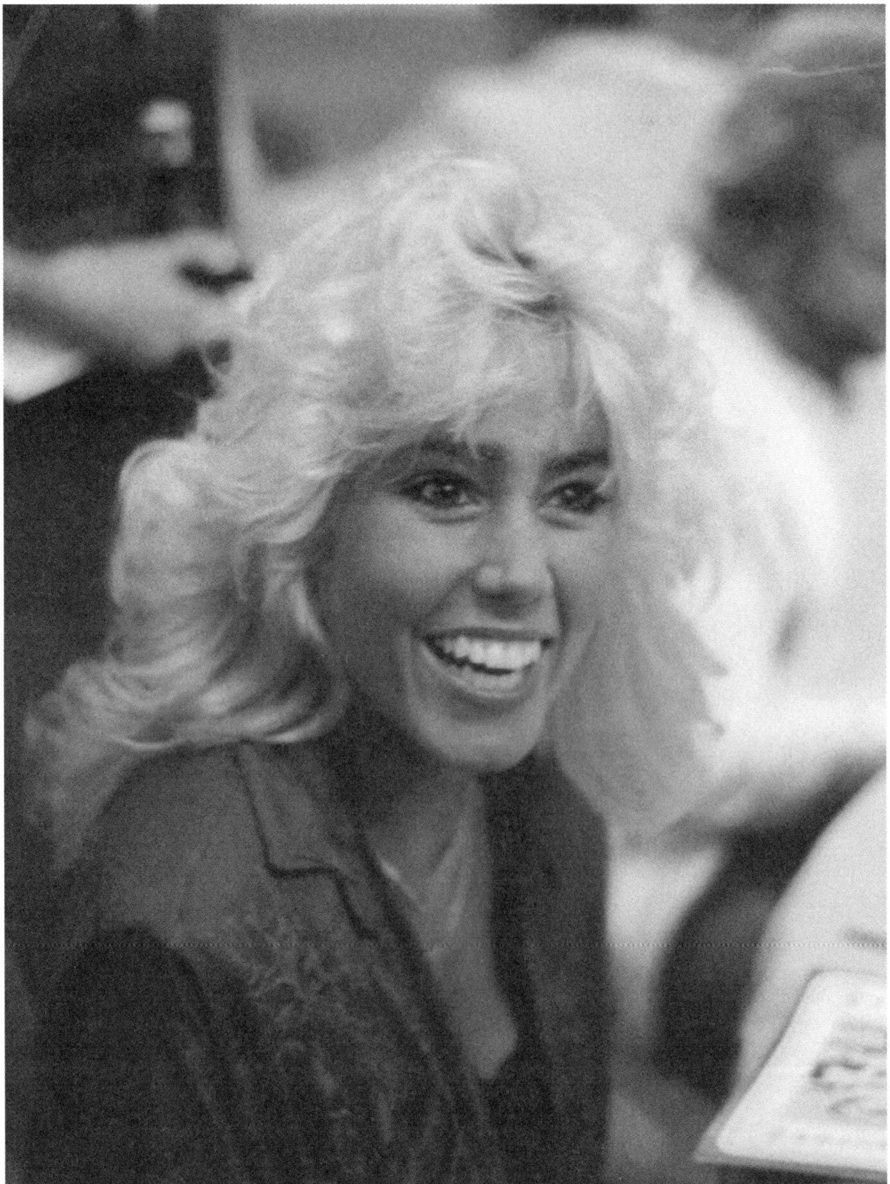

4

Wrestling with the Mania

New York, WWF

Jim Crockett, who owned and promoted the National Wrestling Alliance out of the Carolinas, bought the UWF from Bill Watts in 1987. Crockett was rolling in dough and looking to keep pace with Vince McMahon's WWF in the northeast by dominating the south and southwest markets. The rumor going around the locker room was that he planned to keep the NWA and the UWF as separate entities — which meant, or so we thought, two things. First, that our old contracts with Watts would be voided. And second, that he planned to offer most of us new contracts under Crockett Promotions.

Still, that's the kind of news that shakes up an organization, and from the moment Crockett began to close in on the UWF deal, people from the front office to the stage hands were running scared. Eddie and I were pretty sure we were safe. I mean, Eddie was wrestling, managing and booking, so he was like a bargain. And I was . . . well, I was Missy. But all the same, I sent our photographs to the WWF.

Then, one Friday afternoon, Eddie and I were hanging around my apartment in Baton Rouge. I remember I was tanning in the sun bed — John and I had invested in one when we lived together, and I got custody of it, finally, after a long fight, when we split up. The telephone rang. The phone was right next to the sun bed, so I answered it. But I was like half asleep.

So I'm lying there in the sun bed, with my little black goggles on, and I bring the receiver to my head, and I yawn real loud, and then finally I say, "Hello?"

It's a man's voice. "Hello, is this Missy Hyatt?"

"Yeah."

I yawn again.

"Am I calling at a bad time?"

"No, who is this?"

"This is Vince McMahon."

Suddenly, I'm gasping for air. My heart's pounding, and I'm trying to wedge open the sun bed and climb out. Except I can't unhook the latch without putting down the phone, and I don't want to put down the phone because I'm afraid he'll hang up. So I'm banging the receiver into the latch, then yelling in the phone, "Sorry! I'll be right with you!" then grabbing for the latch again until I finally got it to open.

Then I'm like, "Hello, Mr. McMahon, are you still there?"

"I'm still here," he says. "You sent me some pictures."

"Yeah, that's me!"

"Well, I'd like to talk about your future."

Now Eddie was taking out the garbage, and at that moment I heard him come back into the apartment. Eddie had worked for Vince in the early 1980's, as a protégé of Bob Backlund, until Eddie injured his neck, so I knew that he and Vince knew each other. I tried to wave to Eddie, to put him on the phone, but he was getting a beer from the refrigerator and didn't notice me. Meanwhile, I was hyperventilating after the struggle to climb out of the sun bed. I mean, it was *Vince McMahon!* The WWF! Wrestlemania! So finally, I managed to spit out, "Hey, do you want to speak to Eddie? He just came in."

I didn't give him a chance to answer; I just called Eddie over to the phone.

He was looking at me like I was crazy.

I put my hand over the receiver. "Vince McMahon . . . it's Vince McMahon! He's on the phone! Vince McMahon!"

And Eddie looks at me and rolls his eyes, like, *Yeah, right.*

I hand the phone to him, and he says hello, and then his eyes open real wide, but his voice is calm the entire time. By the end of the conversation, Eddie is nodding his head, and I'm thinking, "Oh my God! Oh my

God! We're going to New York! We're doing Wrestlemania!"

Then I heard Eddie tell Vince, "Well, we've got a couple of days off right now. How about tomorrow?"

Vince flew us up to New York City the next morning. The connections took half the day — from Baton Rouge to Memphis and then, after a three hour layover, on to Laguardia Airport. But it was the first time I'd ever flown first class, so I didn't mind. I'd never seen Eddie as psyched. The whole way up, he was talking about how we were going to be the star couple of the WWF. See, we'd read in the *Wrestling Observer* that Roddy Piper was leaving the organization, so Eddie figured that Vince had in mind for him to take over as host of Piper's Pit — which was their television interview segment. And he figured that Vince wanted me for a feud with Miss Elizabeth. I mean, it seemed like a perfect fit for both of us.

During the layover in Memphis, Eddie talked my ear off about how he was planning to change Piper's Pit; he kept coming up with new names for the segment. I remember one of them was "Gilbert's Grapevine." He would change the set to look like a vineyard. He was like a little kid.

There was a black limousine waiting for us at the airport. I'd never been to New York City before, but there was no time to sightsee. The driver took us straight to WWF offices in Connecticut.

As soon as we step out of the car, Vince is waiting for us outside the front door. Eddie walks in front to shake his hand. Vince is real friendly to him; he's patting Eddie on the shoulder, saying how glad he is to see him again. But even while they're shaking hands, Vince is already looking past Eddie and straight at me.

So I step forward to shake his hand.

The first words Vince McMahon says to me are: "Young lady, *you* are going to be a star."

And I'm like, "Huh?"

"You're going to host Piper's Pit. But we'll call it something else. *Missy's Manor* is what we have in mind, but that's tentative. We can play around with it if you come up with something better. You're going to be the next Hulk Hogan, young lady. We're going to make you as big as the Hulkster!"

Out of the corner of my eye, I see Eddie's shoulders sagging.

Meanwhile, Vince is going on and on. "We're going to pay for your clothes. You're going to need bodyguards wherever you go. You're never going to be able to shop at a grocery store again."

Finally, he turns back around to Eddie. "And don't think I've forgotten that the two of you come as a package. Whatever you want to do, Eddie . . . you want to wrestle, you want to manage, whatever you prefer is fine. Hey, if you decide to manage, you can bring in whoever you want. You were working with tag teams, right?"

But then he turns to me again.

"You're going to have a doll, young lady. We're going to put out a Missy Doll. And that doll is going to wind up on the dresser of every thirteen year old girl in the world. We've got marketing people here who are going to make it all happen."

Now *that* got to me.

I remember thinking: Eddie's upset . . . I know he's upset . . . I know he had his heart set on doing Piper's Pit . . . *But oh my God, I'm going to have a doll! Oh my God, a Missy Doll! Oh my God! Oh my God! Oh my God!*

I didn't look at Eddie the rest of the afternoon.

On the plane ride back, Eddie was miserable. He was trying not to show it, trying to pretend he was happy for my sake, but he never could put up much of a front. Eddie was always the kind of guy whose eyes gave him away. Like whatever he felt was welling up inside his eyes, just about to spill over. He had no poker face.

Finally, he said, "I didn't tell you this before, but Ken gave notice last week, and Crockett offered me the booking job with the UWF. I think I'm going to take it."

"But what about Vince? What about New York?"

"I think I'd rather book," he said. "But you go ahead."

Then I started to cry. "I don't want to go without you."

He got a serious expression on his face, a moment-of-truth kind of expression. His voice got real low. "Look, honey, I'm not going to hold you back. You go do your thing. You go get that doll."

That just made it worse, the fact that he was being so sympathetic. "But what about *us?*"

"We'll be okay," he said. "It's not like we won't see each other. We'll just rack up frequent flyer miles."

I met Jim Crockett for the first time a couple of days later. He was a short stocky guy with glasses; he looked like a cross between an accountant and a used car salesman. The first thing I said to him, word for word, was: "Hi, I'm Missy Hyatt. I want out of my contract."

He didn't look surprised. He smiled at me. "All right, if you want out of your contract, you're out of it."

"No, no, it's not like that," I said. "See, Vince McMahon offered me a deal with the WWF. They want to bring me up to New York. They're going to make me a *doll!*"

He just kept on smiling and asked if Eddie was going too, and I said no — Eddie still intended to stay on as the UWF booker. So he only nodded and said fine. End of story. But as I was about to leave his office, he told me that I'd better talk to Bill Watts since their deal hadn't gone through yet, so, technically, I was still under contract to Watts.

Now Bill Watts never liked me very much. His teenage son Eric had a major crush on me, and I used to wink at him and then ask him to do my laundry. But I was like that; it was a Missy-type thing to do. I mean, who did it hurt? I'm sure the kid went home afterwards and told all his friends how Missy Hyatt had the hots for him.

But Eric's father, Cowboy Bill Watts, always intimidated me. First of all, he was just a huge guy, six foot six inches, 300 pounds. Second of all, he had a real bad temper. He was once wrestling a Russian guy named Korchenko. Korchenko was a guy Eddie brought in to manage, and the feud with Watts was supposed to be Korchenko's big break, his first major storyline — you know, the Communist versus the Cowboy. The set up was that Korchenko crept up behind Watts during an interview and knocked him out, and then he laid the Soviet flag across his body. That led up their first match in Jackson, Mississippi. Except Korchenko must have said something to him beforehand, maybe asked for more money, because Watts, who was known for being a shooter anyway, went into the ring and stretched him. Locked him down with one hold after another, the kind that can make you barf, and he wouldn't let loose. The entire match, Watts was whispering to him. Afterwards, Korchenko ran out of the ring, out of the building, jumped in his car where his wife was waiting — and he never wrestled again. No one ever found out what happened to him. He left his gym bag in the locker.

So I went to Bill Watts office in Tulsa, and I told him that I wanted out of my contract.

He said no.

He didn't raise his voice. He just sat behind his desk, heard me out, and then shook his head. I guess he must have known beforehand that I had an offer from Vince McMahon, who he flat out hated, and he decided to screw with both of us.

I was stunned. I said, "But you're selling out to Crockett."

"That's not official yet. It won't be for a couple of months. Until then, I own you."

"Well, I won't work for you."

"Then you won't get paid. Meanwhile, you won't work for anyone else."

"You can't do that. I can work for whoever I want."

He leaned forward over the desk. "Maybe *you* can. But *Missy* can't."

"What's that supposed to mean?"

"*Missy Hyatt* is intellectual property. I own exclusive rights to her services. McMahon may get you, but he won't get Missy."

"*Missy Hyatt* is my name! It's who I am!"

"You're *Melissa Hiatt*. You want to work for McMahon under that name, God bless you. But Missy *Hyatt* stays with the UWF."

Well, I left Watts's office in tears, and I called Vince McMahon and told him what had happened. Vince put his wife, Linda, who was an attorney, on the phone, and she told me not to worry. *Missy Hyatt* was a name, not intellectual property, so no one could stop me from using it. They flew me up first class again the next week to sign forms and do photos and promos, and afterwards Linda contacted Jim Crockett. The two of them talked, and then Crockett talked to Watts, and then, finally, Watts gave in. But, just as a final dig, he fined me freaking $500 for missing a couple of UWF shows.

Unbelievable.

That episode taught me an important lesson though. I went out and got my name registered and trademarked — just in case someone else ever tried to take it from me. Oh, and years later I fucked Bill Watts's son Eric and then made him do my laundry one last time.

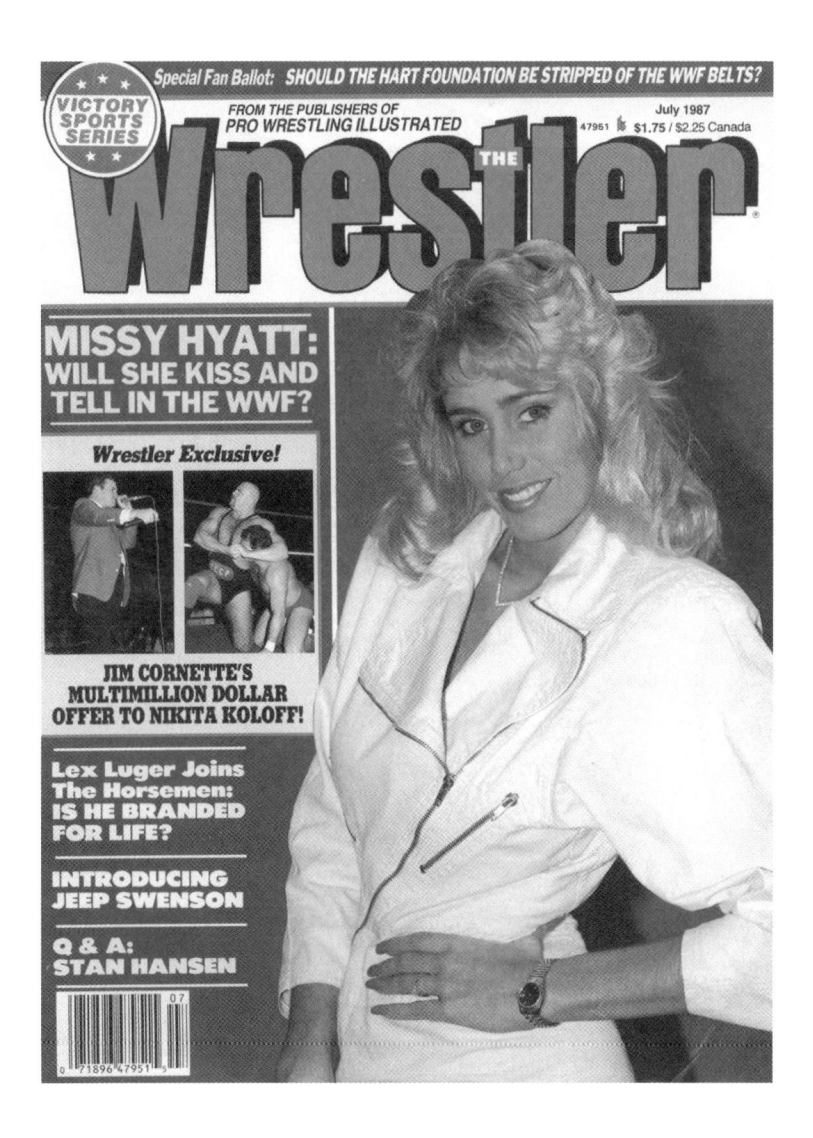

How do you like that, Cowboy?

🍸

My final appearance for the UWF, a week before I left for the WWF, was in the four girl Battle Royal in Atlanta. It was Baby Doll, Sunshine, Dark Journey and me. Eddie scripted it for me to be eliminated first by Sunshine; I mean, I wasn't going to take a chance on getting hurt, and I knew Sunshine would look out for me. But I had payback on my mind with Dark Journey for all the times she beat my ass. The day before the match, Eddie was trying to teach me how to take her down shoot style. Put her in an abdominal stretch till she barfed. I thought I had it too. But the night of the Battle Royal, I couldn't get a grip on her. She was too greasy. I think she put on lotion or something. I was so frustrated. I kept jumping on her, trying to roll her over into an abdominal stretch, and she kept squirting loose, and meanwhile Sunshine is chasing both of us around the ring, wondering why I'm not following the match.

Finally, Sunshine gave me a look like, *What the hell's going on?* Then she grabbed me by the hair, the way we planned, and was about to pin me. But just before she threw me down, I got in one good kick to Dark Journey who was rolling around on the mat with Baby Doll. I was wearing tennis shoes, and I kicked her so hard, I broke my baby toe.

As I limped back to the dressing room, I was screaming back to her, "Go ahead and say something, bitch! Eddie's the booker now! Say something! You're nobody in this business! You're nobody, and I'm getting a Missy Doll!"

Eddie's divorce from Teri was finalized in 1987, and we got engaged. We had no definite plans for a wedding, just a determination that we would stay together, no matter what.

The McMahons put me up in a beautiful hotel in Connecticut, picked me up in a limousine every morning — and for the first week, it was a like a blitz of photo-sessions and clothes-shopping. They ran a spread on me in the WWF magazine, and I taped a 30-second spot for their TV show. I still remember that spot. It started with a shot of a man's shoes and a voice-over: "People have been wondering who's going to fill Roddy Piper's shoes, what man could possibly do the job. . . ." Then the camera suddenly cut to a pair of black high heels and started panning up real slow, from the calves to the thighs to the hem of a short leather skirt. Then the voice-over started up again. "Well, it's not going to be a man. It's going to be a woman. All woman. Missy Hyatt is coming to the WWF . . . and the wrestling world will never be the same."

Vince bought me an entire wardrobe, all leather, all skin-tight. It was

With a well-known mark, Tom Arnold

a slight shift in the character, you know, like a hint of fetish. When I first started, I used to wear pink tennis outfits to play off the rich socialite persona. Then I started to alternate between tennis outfits and spandex, still kind of like an aerobics mode, with occasional leather accessories — but only because I thought leather was classy and sexy. But once I got to the WWF, I wanted all leather, all the time.

Hey, Vince was buying.

The first episodes of "Missy's Manor" were set to be taped in Las Vegas at the UNLV Center. Vince flew me out the night before the show. Again, it was nothing but first class. There was a limo waiting at the airport to take me to Bally's Hotel where Vince and his entourage were staying. I checked in at the front desk, turn around, and suddenly, out of nowhere, there's a guy waiting behind me. He puts out his hand and says, "Hi, I'm Dick. I'm a friend of Vince's. I do Saturday Night's Main Event with him."

I smile at him and shake his hand. "Oh, really? That's nice. Here, can you carry this?"

Then I hand him my Louis Vuitton luggage.

He smiles at me kind of funny, but he takes the bags, and the two of us stop by Vince's suite before heading up to mine.

Vince is waiting for us inside.

So this Dick guy sets down the bags, and then he turns to Vince and says, "The lady's got expensive taste in luggage."

Meanwhile, I'm thinking, *Yeah, whatever. Just be careful with the freaking bags.*

Vince gives me his usual big, "Hi." Then I nod at Dick and kind of whisper in Vince's ear, "Do you tip him or do I?"

That just cracks Vince up. Next thing I know, he and Dick are both laughing.

"Missy, I'd like you to meet Dick Ebersol."

And I'm like, "Yeah, I know. We met in the lobby."

That cracks them up again. But I don't think much about it. I figure it's just a guy thing, or else maybe it's a joke about the Vuitton luggage that I'm not getting. Vince tells me that a group of WWF people are going out for a night on the town, and he'd like me to join them. Actually, what I really want at that point is a nap, but I figure it's not a good idea to say no to Vince, so I tell him I'll meet him downstairs in a half hour.

There were about ten people in the lobby when I came downstairs. Vince. Dick Ebersol. Mean Gene Okerlund. Rene Goulet. Plus, wives and friends. No one else that I can remember though. We walk over to Caesar's Palace where there's a private table reserved for us, and we settle down for a nine course meal. The image that stays in my mind is the wine guys pouring wine over our shoulders; I remember thinking what a silly skill that was, being able to pour wine out of a spouted canister and into a glass three feet below. But I kept gulping it down.

After dinner, we stuck around for the stage show. The headliners were Sammy Davis Jr. and Jerry Lewis. The entire time, mind you, I'm still thinking Dick Ebersol is just Vince's lackey because he's flitting around, setting stuff up for us, reserving a special table, ordering hors d'oeuvres carts, making sure we're happy. Finally, he comes running back to the table as the show is about to end and says, "C'mon, we're going backstage!"

So we walk backstage, and the first person Dick introduces us to is Jerry Lewis. He's sitting in his dressing room in a satin *I'm-a-star* robe, you know, with a big *JL* monogrammed across the breast pocket. He talked to us for a few minutes, just your basic small talk. "How'd you like the show?" "Oh, it was great." Stuff like that.

Then Dick took us to meet Sammy. The second we walk in, he jumps up from his chair and starts yelling. "Vince McMahon! My main man! Man, I dig what you're doing!" Then Sammy turns to me and he slaps his cheek, like he can't believe it. "You're Missy Hyatt, aren't you? You are *hot*, baby."

I almost fainted.

Then he turns back to Vince. "Hey, man, I want to be part of the next Wrestlemania. Whatever you want me to do, I'm there, man."

Vince just nods his head and smiles.

Then we leave, but we're not ten steps out of the casino when Vince turns to the rest of us and says, "Everybody wants to be part of Wrestlemania. But you know what? We don't need him!" Then he bursts out laughing, this loud booming laugh that echoes up and down the street, and then, a second later, the rest of us start to laugh too.

Then I said to him, as the laughter was dying down, "You know what? You are *so* cool."

And, I mean, he was.

I guess the punchline to that story is that it wasn't until like a month later, when I saw Dick Ebersol with his wife, Susan Saint James, that I realized he was more than just Vince's flunkie. But I didn't figure out how much more until years later, when I read in *USA Today* that Dick Ebersol had just been named head of NBC Sports.

If I'd known that beforehand, I would've tipped him real well for carrying my luggage.

The following afternoon, I hopped another limo out to the UNLV Center to tape the first segment of Missy's Manor. I was supposed to tape between that night's matches. The show wasn't even due to start until eight o'clock, but I arrived hours ahead of time to get a feel for the place. Vince had built a special set for me, a huge pink couch with fluffy pillows, and the opening shot was a pink heart that read, *Missy's Manor*. As I was strolling across the set, Vince showed up with Hulk Hogan. It was the first time I'd ever met Hogan, and there's no way to prepare yourself. I mean, the guy is gigantic. I don't mean just his body. I mean his persona. His charisma. Even his voice is huge. He was already in his wrestling tights, and his shoulders looked like cooked hams. Plus, he didn't have a single hair on his arms or legs. Not even a trace of stubble. His skin was just bare. Like cooked ham.

So Vince brings him over to me and says, "Missy, I'd like you to meet the Hulkster."

We shake hands, and I don't know what to say.

Then Hogan says, "So, I hear you've come to take my spot."

Vince slaps him on the shoulder. "Not *take* it, Hulkster. Just share it for a while."

Hogan stares down at me and grins. "So you think you're up to it?"

"I don't know, Hulk," I say. "Your chest is way bigger than mine."

He got a good laugh out of it. Vince gave me the thumbs up as he and Hogan headed off to the dressing room.

The program started right on time, 8:00. The UNLV Center was sold out, and I was standing backstage through the first three matches. I was a nervous wreck; my throat was so tight I had to keep drinking water to swallow. Then, finally, I heard Howard Finkel, the ring announcer, say, "Ladies and Gentlemen, it's time for Missy's Manor." And there's like this loud "Huh?" that comes from the crowd. I mean, at that point, all I'd done in the WWF was shoot a few promos. That was it. The only people who really knew who I was, or what I did, were WCCW and UWF fans. But this was Nevada, not Texas or Tennessee. I'd never worked a show west of Oklahoma before. I don't think even half the crowd had ever heard my name.

There was about a half second pause between Howard Finkel's introduction and the moment I appeared from behind the curtains. I was used to hearing screams and curses as soon as my name was announced. But that night I remember just this awkward deafening silence as I walked onto the Missy's Manor set. I had on a tight pink leather dress and pink leather shoes and even pink leather earrings; my hair was cut in wing-backed Farrah Fawcett style. (I still cringe whenever I see a photograph from that show!) No one knew how to react, so I realized right off that I had to establish the character. I introduced myself again, and then I said, "So how do you like my dress? Don't you think it's sexy? Do you want to see more?" I did a quick catwalk spin, and by then the crowd was starting to boo. "C'mon, guys, you know you want to see more of my manor. . . ." Suddenly, the men were cheering and the women were booing even louder.

I felt the nervousness fade away: I was Missy again.

The trouble was, as soon as I finished the introduction, I had to sit down on the couch and do an interview. I mean, I'd taped hundreds of interviews with WCCW and UWF; but I was always the interviewee, not the interviewer.

Turns out it's not as easy as it looks.

The first guests I had were Honky Tonk Man and his manager Jimmy Hart. They walk onto the set, and Honky Tonk looks me up and down and says, "*Mercy*, you're looking good, baby!" Then the two of them sit down on the couch next to me. So now I'm holding the microphone, and I ask Honky Tonk something like where he buys his clothes. I remember, as I was asking him the question, I was thinking, *What a stupid question! I can't believe I just asked him that!*

Then I lean back and wait for him to answer.

The problem is Honky Tonk isn't miked. I'm supposed to lean forward and put the microphone under his chin for his answer, but instead I just lean back, taking the microphone back with me, and I wait for an answer.

He just stares at me with this panicky look. Meanwhile, Jimmy Hart is waving frantically, trying to catch my eye, trying to get me to move the mike towards him.

Pink leather with Farrah hair

I figure maybe he didn't hear the question, so I lean forward again and repeat it. "I'm sure all your fans are wondering where you shop for your clothes, Honky Tonk."

Then I lean back again with the mike.

Finally, Honky Tonk reaches over to me and pulls the microphone forward. "Missy, I'd rather talk about what me and you are going to do later tonight, but it seems like you're just like the rest of these people — you want to know all the personal stuff. Well, I got this shop down in Memphis that makes my clothes special for me. Now tell the truth, little lady, you're not interested in my clothes, are you? You want to run your hands through my hair, don't you?"

And I'm like, "Sorry, Honky Tonk, I'm not into that greasy kid stuff. . . . But now tell me this. I see you with that guitar all the time, but I never hear you play it. Why is that?"

Now Honky Tonk's staring at me, like, *What?*

Finally, Jimmy Hart leans forward and grabs the microphone and pulls it towards him, and he say, "Missy Hyatt, I know you're like all the rest of the women in the world. You want to get next to the Honky Tonk Man. I see how you're making eyes at him. I have to guard his hotel room every night against women like you. . . ."

And then he was off. He pretty much did the rest of the interview on his own. It was like a three-minute monologue, with Jimmy Hart talking, and Honky Tonk nodding, and me just kind of smiling and holding the mike and waiting for the segment to finish.

I mean, afterwards, I just wanted to crawl off that set and die.

Vince told me not to worry about bombing out on the first segment. He was real nice; he even said he should have used a boom mike for the segment.

But the thing was, it wasn't just the microphone. It was the entire concept. Missy doing interviews. There was a flaw in the logic of it, an inconsistency between who Missy was and what she was doing. I mean, in Missy's mind, the world revolves around her. She's not interested in what anyone else has to say. Still, I did a few more interviews.

It was out in Anaheim, California, six weeks later, that Vince took me aside and said, "The Missy's Manor bit isn't really going the way we want. It's no reflection on you. We're going to come up with another gimmick for you."

I understood what he was saying; I mean, I'd watched the tapes. But I'd been thinking about it, and I thought I'd come up with an idea to make Missy's Manor work. I would start the interviews straight but then turn them around, like, "Welcome to Missy's Manor, Hulk Hogan. You've got a match coming up next week in Philadelphia against Harley Race. But what your fans *really* want to know about is what do you think about my new haircut?"

But I was just too intimidated. I didn't speak up. Vince said he had another gimmick for me, so I just nodded my head and bit my lip.

The gimmick Vince had come up with was for me to become a Federette. They were the girls who walked to the ring with the wrestlers and then took off their monogrammed robes. I mean, it wasn't even like being a valet. Vince promised that I would be like the lead Federette. He would work out an storyline where Honky Tonk Man keeps hitting on me, and I wind up slapping him in the face. But when I asked him where the angle would go after the slap, he just shrugged.

Meanwhile, Eddie was still booking for Jim Crockett in the UWF, and I was going crazy flying back and forth from New York to Dallas. When I told him what was happening in the WWF, he was like, "Hey, honey, don't do that. You're Missy Hyatt. You're no Federette. You don't walk out to the ring with three other girls in the same outfit. You're one of a kind." He also blew up when I mentioned that Vince wanted me to work with Honky Tonk Man. He wouldn't explain why; he was real mysterious about it. But he was dead set against me and Honky Tonk working together. I mean, Eddie put up with me still managing John Tatum even after I'd left John for him. But for some reason, the thought of me working with Honky Tonk just got under his skin.

I never did find out what it was about Honky Tonk Man that drove Eddie up the wall. Maybe it had to do with the fact that the two of them were from Tennessee, maybe something happened way back. Maybe it was a chick. *Something* must have happened between them. I know if I'd told Eddie that Vince wanted me to work with Hulk Hogan, or with Macho Man and Elizabeth, Eddie would have been all for it.

But towards the end of the conversation, Eddie was done yelling. He told me to come home; he would talk to Dusty, and I could get my old job back.

So, basically, I left the WWF after two months because I was in love with Eddie Gilbert, and because I didn't want to work the new gimmick Vince McMahon had worked up. You can list the two reasons in whatever order you like. But they added up to me telling Vince thanks but no thanks. I was up front about it; I told him Eddie didn't want me to be a Federette. He nodded his head like he understood. He was real sweet about it. He was sweet about everything, truthfully. He said that he was sorry things didn't work out. "Maybe the time's not right for you," he said. "Eddie's telling you one thing, and I'm telling you another thing, and of course you've got to follow your heart." But he told me to call him if I ever wanted to give the WWF another shot.

Plus, he let me keep all the leather clothes: I *still* have a couple of those outfits!

Eventually, I did call Vince back — practically begged on my hands and knees for a job. But that was years later, like 1997. The bad thing about the WWF back then was that no one in the organization had a clue how to use women. They would come up with an angle for a woman, then bring in someone who fit the physical type. That's backwards. The angle has to flow from the character. I think Sunny, really, was the first woman who got the right kind of push from the WWF — you know, they got to know her, then worked around who she was. (Actually, there's a lot of Missy in Sunny!) But Sunny didn't turn up until like six years after I was there. After Sunny came Sable, who just went through the roof, and after that they kind of got the hang of it.

But you know what ripped my heart out? The first time I was walking through a Walmart and spotted a Sable Doll. Broke down and started flinging the dolls down the aisles. The store manager asked me to leave.

Because I never did get my Missy Doll.

Bastards!

Happy together – Eddie and me

As for Vince McMahon, well, what can I say? I'd rag on him if I could, but the truth is the truth. He treated me like a princess, gave me every chance to do well, but I was too green, and I flopped. Like Stone Cold says, "That's the bottom line."

About the only bad thing I have to say about Vince is that he had panty lines. Not *literally*. I don't know what they're called on men. He wore expensive tailored suits, I mean, like five thousand dollar suits, but from behind you could always see the outline of his underwear and how his shirt tail was bunched up and tucked in below his belt.

That always skeeved me about Vince.

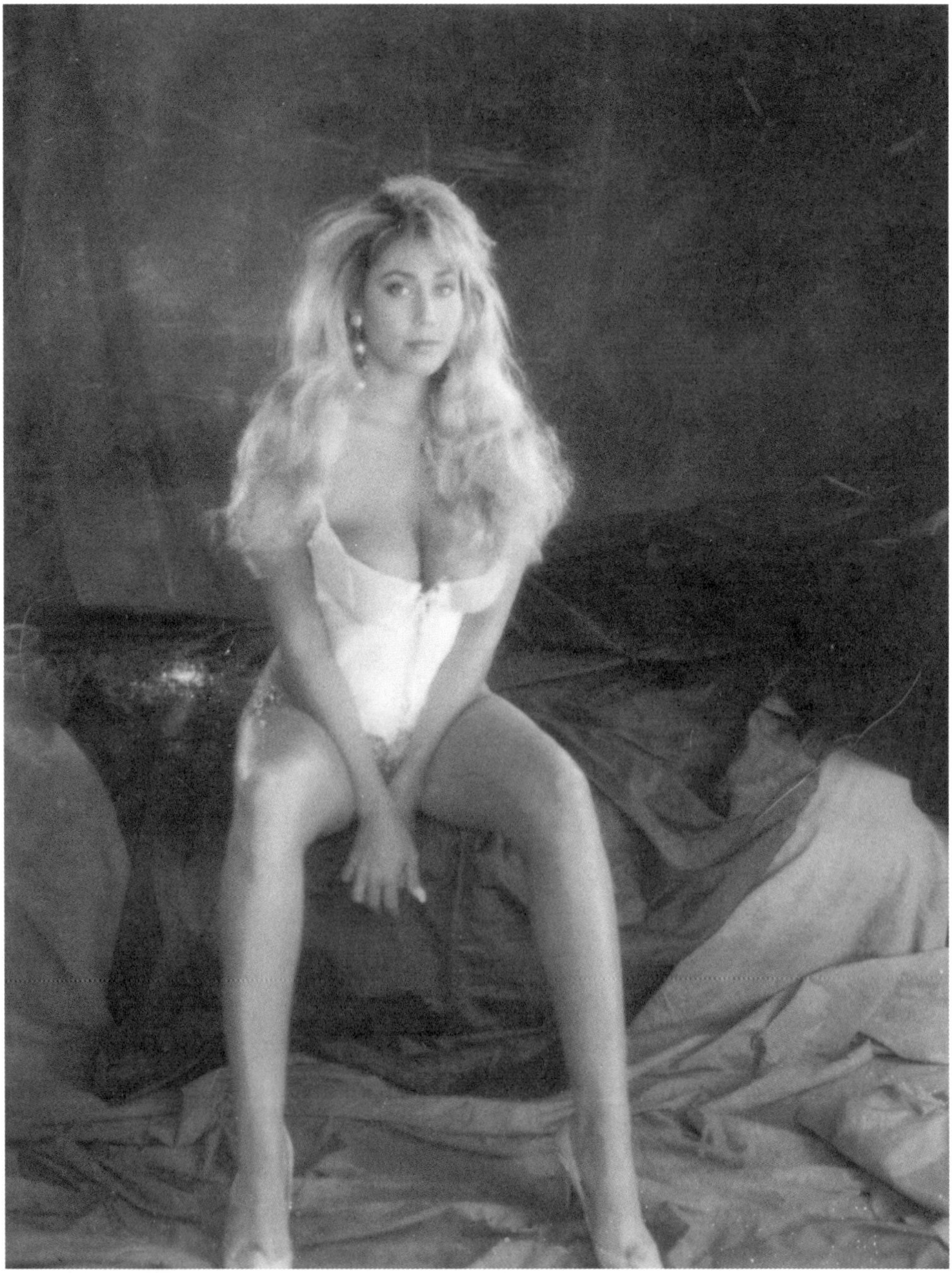

5

Ain't No Place I'd Rather Be

Oklahoma and Tennessee, UWF/NWA and USWA

During the time I was with WWF, the deal between Bill Watts and Jim Crockett had gone through, and Crockett Promotions had moved the UWF's headquarters from Tulsa to Dallas. So now I had to slink back into Jim Crockett's Dallas office — remember, it's only four months since I told him I wanted out of my UWF contract — and ask him for a job. I knocked on the office door, and he told me to come in, but then he didn't even look up at me. He was reading a newspaper with his feet up on his desk.

Then I'm like, "Hi, Mr. Crockett. How're you doing?"

That's when he looked up from the newspaper. "Wait . . . I remember you. You're Missy, right? You're that big WWF star?"

Hey, I had it coming. I always liked Jim. He always spoke to me in a nice even tone of voice, and that counts for a lot. Wrestling people tend to be screamers. Jim never wrestled himself, never had a thing to do with the sport actually. His father owned a minor league baseball team and a minor league hockey team, and then he bought a wrestling promotion. It was a business investment. That was how Jim always looked at it. He didn't take things personally the way Bill Watts did.

So I said, "I was wondering if I could have my job back."

"I don't know, Missy."

Then there was like a five-second pause.

Finally, Jim smiled and said, "Eddie told me what happened. Go downstairs and talk to Dusty. He's already working on something for you."

I stepped forward as if to hug him, but he waved me off.

Now Dusty Rhodes used to call me his Jayne Mansfield, so when I walked into his office, he called out, "My Jayne Mansfield, what do you need, baby?" Then he came around his desk and gave me a bear hug.

I mean, he was just so sweet. He said, "Vince didn't know how to use you, baby. Ain't nothing to be ashamed of. Now I'm going to use you right. You're going to co-host the UWF show. You'll be working with Jim Ross. Just be yourself, baby. Nothing more to it than that."

Then he brushed away my tears with his thumbs. It was a real emotional moment, but I remember thinking, "God, he's got fat thumbs!"

So I started to co-host the UWF show with Jim Ross. I'd never announced before, but it was much easier than doing interviews. I didn't have to call moves; that was Jim Ross's job — and he was, and still is, the best in the business. I didn't even have to do analysis. What I had to do was keep the viewers tuned in. Whatever it took. Naturally, I spent most of the time ragging on the babyfaces. Remember, in the UWF, I was still a heel. So Barry Windham would be in a match, and in between Ross calling the moves, I'd chime in with, "I cannot believe Barry Windham thinks those tights match his boots. *Obviously*, he was raised in a low class household. He probably got dressed in front of the pigs and chickens."

So each week I would do the opening of the UWF show, just basic stuff, run down the matches, rag on the wrestlers — that kind of thing. Then I would sit ringside and comment on the matches. And meanwhile I'm still wearing the leather outfits Vince McMahon bought for me.

There was talk every now and then of resurrecting Hot Stuff and Hyatt International, but that would have meant dropping me as an announcer, so I said no. As a matter of fact, Dusty avoided putting me on air with Eddie; he said it would only call attention to the fact that I'd been gone for three months, that I'd run out on the UWF and jumped to the WWF, and

What I wear to bed every night

he didn't want to provide Vince McMahon free publicity. Besides, Eddie wasn't doing much wrestling back then, just an occasional mini-angle, like a two-week feud with Terry Taylor. Otherwise, he was booking full time.

Eventually, Dusty decided to shift me to the Sunday show with Tony Schiavone which ran nationwide on TBS. That was the first cable program I did. Nowadays, people take cable stations like TBS for granted, but back then, going cable was a big deal. I know it made a difference to my folks. Before that, I'd turn up on television at different hours throughout the Midwest and South, anywhere from nine in the morning to after midnight, but the programs always seemed to run at like one in the morning in Tallahassee. My folks didn't bother to tape them; they didn't like watching me get booed. So I'd send them stuff like tapes and clippings every now and then. Truthfully, though, they never wanted to tell their friends what I was doing. I mean, they wouldn't lie about it if someone asked, but my parents would never bring up the subject. Basically, they thought wrestling was so, like, *Ugh*. But when I started the TBS show — well, it's like *I'd* gone prime time. Suddenly, my dad would meet his friends at the hardware store, and he'd be like, "Yeah, that was my daughter on TV last Sunday."

It also made a difference to me, the way I lived, because people knew who I was *everywhere*. It was kind of like what Vince McMahon predicted: every time I stepped out for groceries, I'd wind up signing autographs. It didn't matter what city we were working. Dallas. Memphis. New Orleans. Especially Atlanta — fans there got the UWF's broadcast *and* cable programs, so I was on television three times a week. Whenever we worked Atlanta, we would leave the hotel, and people would be like, "Hey, you're the girl on wrestling."

Eddie and I were always on the verge of getting married, you know, setting dates and phoning reception halls, but the timing never quite worked. The thing was, so many of our friends were wrestlers, meaning they were always on the road, that trying to coordinate schedules got to be like trying to plan the freaking invasion of Kuwait. Lots of times, the two of us talked about just doing it, just running down to a local justice of the peace and telling our friends and folks afterwards — except neither of us wanted that. But no matter what date and what town we settled on, we knew for sure we would wind up hurting a lot of people's feelings.

Well, every year Jim Crockett threw a big Halloween bash for all the NWA and UWF wrestlers. So Eddie and I were sitting around after dinner one night, trying to figure out our costumes for the 1988 party, and then, suddenly, he looked at me kind of funny.

He said, "Why don't we have our own party this year?"

"What about Crockett?"

"Forget Crockett. We'll have our own party, and get dressed up as a bride and groom."

For a second, I thought he was ribbing me; he knew how frustrated I was by the fact that we still weren't married. So I just kind of shot him a look, like, *Hah, hah, very funny.*

But then he said, "No, I mean as a *real* bride and groom. We'll hire a justice of the peace — except he'll come dressed up as something else. We won't tell anyone it's for real except our folks."

I still wasn't sure he was serious. But he swore he was, and the more I thought about it, the more I liked it. I mean, it was such a romantic idea

— a secret wedding with everyone there. Plus, it was also kind of a crazy-daffy idea. It just cracked me up.

We decided to go for it.

Our Halloween party was in Euless, Texas in the clubhouse of our apartment building. Only our families and a couple of friends knew in advance what Eddie and I had planned. My dad dressed up as a Confederate soldier and my mom was hiding behind a frilly white mask. Eddie's mom and dad came in costume too — I think his father was a hunchback and his mom was wearing fangs. Terry and Trudy Taylor knew what was going on because they were the best man and maid of honor; they came as a sheik and a belly dancer. Sting and his wife showed up as Barney and Betty Rubble. It was like that. No band, just a friend as the deejay. Mostly, it was just lots of food and alcohol and wrestlers butting heads and laughing.

The justice of the peace showed up half way through the party dressed as a wizard with a pointy black hat and a magic wand and big medallion hanging around his neck. When he walked in, the rest of the guests were like, *Who the hell is that?* — I mean, because pro wrestling is a such tight community that everyone pretty much knows everyone else. So people stared for a minute or so, then forgot about him.

But then, like ten minutes later, the wizard walks to the front, and then Eddie calls for quiet, and he and I line up in front of the wizard in our wedding costumes. Then the Taylors step up behind us, and then our families fall in line behind them.

The second the wizard began to speak, people realized what was going on, and they started to applaud and laugh.

The entire event was videotaped — so, of course, there are bootleg copies still circulating among wrestling fans; I don't have a copy myself though. So if anybody out there's got one. . . .

The weeks right before and right after our wedding were probably the happiest time Eddie and I spent in the UWF. Things started to go downhill afterwards. Jim Crockett decided to fold the UWF into the NWA — which meant that Eddie would have to clear all his booking ideas with Dusty Rhodes. It wasn't that Eddie didn't respect Dusty; there was never the

Scott Levy . . . who later became Scotty the Body . . . who later became Johnny Polo . . . who later became Scotty Flamingo . . . who finally became Raven

slightest animosity between them. They just had two different styles of booking. Dusty was always more of a traditionalist — good guys are good guys and bad guys are bad guys, you know, keep it in the ring and don't confuse the paying customers; whereas Eddy always wanted to do more experimental stuff — like scripting storylines where you're never quite sure who's the babyface and who's the heel. He also liked extreme stuff. Wrestlers getting attacked from behind on their way to the ring.

Matches that spill out of the ring and wind up on the street outside the arena.

Eddie also thought Dusty favored the NWA guys he'd been working with all along over the UWF guys Eddie had been building up on his own. The NWA guys would get the pushes, the interview times, the title shots, and meanwhile the UWF wrestlers wound up working mid-card. It reached the point where Eddie wanted out, and in 1988, he got an offer from Jerry Lawler to come over to Memphis to wrestle and book for the United States Wrestling Association.

No way Eddie was going to turn down that job. First off, he was born in Lexington, Tennessee, so working in Memphis was like going home. Second, Lawler was his boyhood idol. And third, Lawler liked the gimmicky, extreme stuff that Dusty Rhodes never wanted to do.

It was a definite step down, though, professionally. Less money. No cable exposure. Still, Memphis was probably the most wrestling-crazy city in the United States. I mean, the entire town would grind to a halt every Saturday morning when we broadcast live. We used to run a 22 rating — which meant like eleven out of every ten homes were tuned in.

Memphis was where, for the first time, I kind of developed an attitude — I mean, even when I wasn't in character. The fact that I'd been with Vince McMahon and the WWF, and then with UWF on TBS, and now I was back doing a local show . . . well, it got to me. What can I say? I told you at the start there's a lot of Missy in Melissa. She came out in Memphis.

I was a major prima donna.

I'm talking real hissy stuff. Like, for instance, after I got hooked on *Knot's Landing*, I refused to work spot shows on Thursday nights. That kind of thing. I mean, I could have worked the matches and just videotaped *Knot's*, no problem, but I liked watching it live . . . and I was Missy, so that was that. I flat out refused to work Thursday nights.

Lucky thing *Knot's Landing* was never shifted to Monday. That was the night we'd work the big show at Memphis Coliseum. I mean, this was the house The King built — not Elvis! Jerry "The King" Lawler. It was insane how much those people loved wrestling.

The USWA was a different style than the UWF or WWF. It was over the top, real gimmicky. They'd book matches where the loser had to eat dog food (which was never *really* dog food by the way, just corned beef hash with an Alpo label). Or where the manager of one of the wrestlers would be locked in a cage suspended over the ring. Lots of hardcore stuff too. Really, the USWA was the first organization in America to do the kind of extreme matches that were going on in Japan. Ladder matches. Leather strap matches. Barbed wire matches. Even nowadays, when major organizations book gimmick matches, you sometimes hear the wrestlers in the locker room mumbling, "Here comes more Tennessee Bullshit!"

Like I said, it was Jerry Lawler's company. His partner was Jerry Jarrett. We used to call them the Jerrys. I guess the main reason the two Jerrys went in for that kind of stuff was they couldn't afford major stars. No Hulk Hogan. No Ric Flair. No Roddy Piper. They had Jerry Jarrett's son, Jeff Jarrett, who later became The Chosen One with WCW. But back then he was just the boss's son. They also had Lord Humongous for a while . . . who later became Sid Vicious. They had a babyface jobber named Scott Levy . . . who later became Scotty the Body . . . who later became Johnny Polo . . . who later became Scotty Flamingo . . . who finally became Raven.

Actually, Eddie and I worked a mini-angle with Scotty — which was unusual since he was just a jobber back then. Eddie was in the middle of a long feud with Lawler, and Scotty was about the same height and build as Eddie, so we put him in a mask one night and had him sit next to me at ringside, during one of Jerry Lawler's matches, pretending to be Eddie. So, naturally, Lawler spends the entire match gesturing towards the masked guy, begging him to come into the ring and fight. Then Eddie comes running out from the dressing room in a mask . . . and now the crowd's glancing back and forth, wondering what's going on, because it looks like there are two Eddies. Then the real Eddie sneaks up behind Lawler and "throws fire" at him — with flash paper. Now Eddie pulls off his mask, and Scotty pulls off his mask, and the crowd figures out what happened and starts to boo like crazy.

The next week, Lance Russell, the announcer, asks Scotty why he did it, why he sided with Eddie against Jerry Lawler, and Scotty's like, "Missy promised me a date."

So Lance Russell stares at him, like, *What an idiot!* Then he says, "But she's married to Eddie Gilbert! Haven't you ever heard of Hot Stuff and Hyatt? She's not going out on a date with you!"

Then I come running out and tell Scotty, "All right, I'll go out on a date with you . . . if you can beat Jerry Lawler in the ring right now."

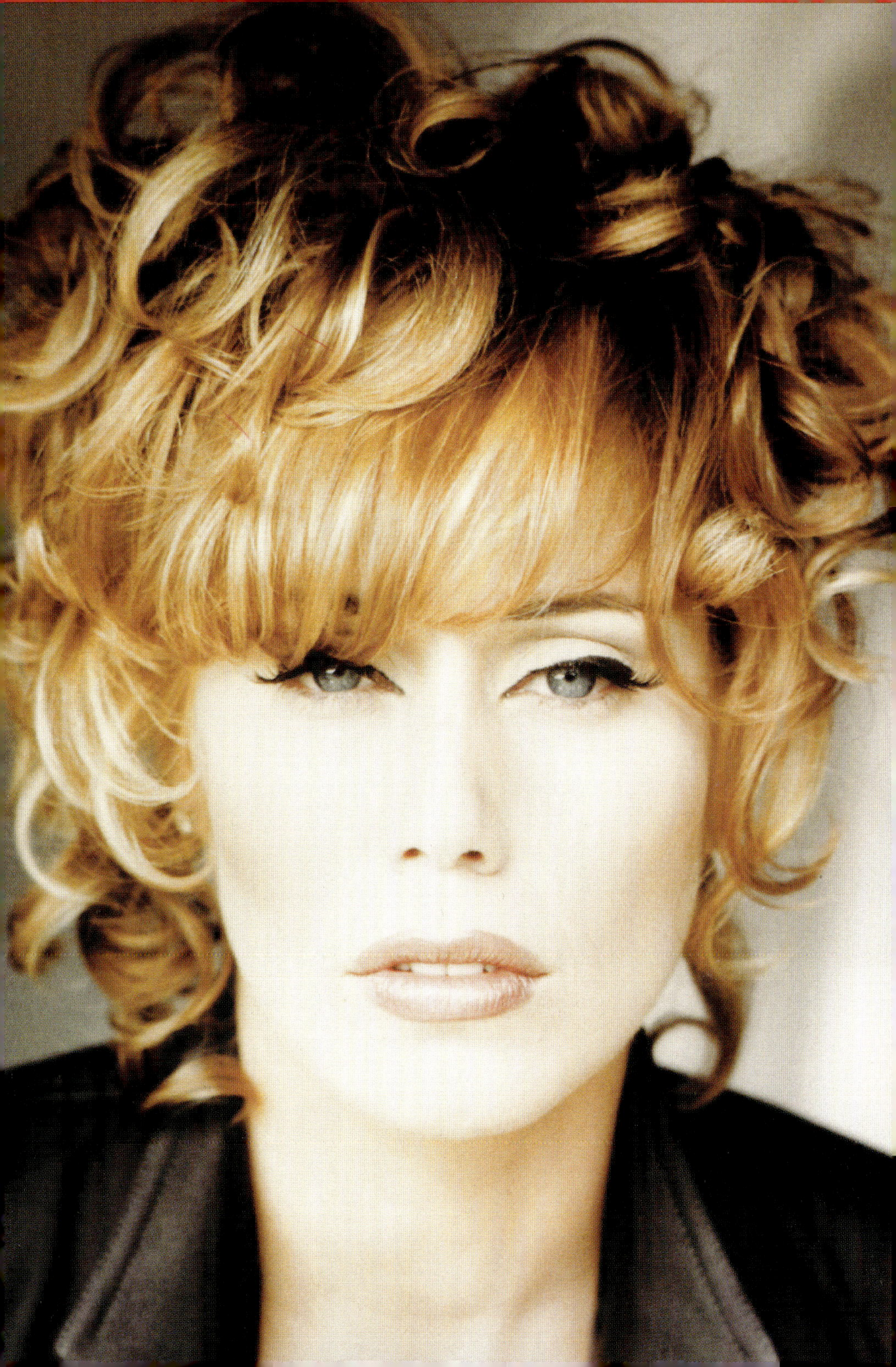

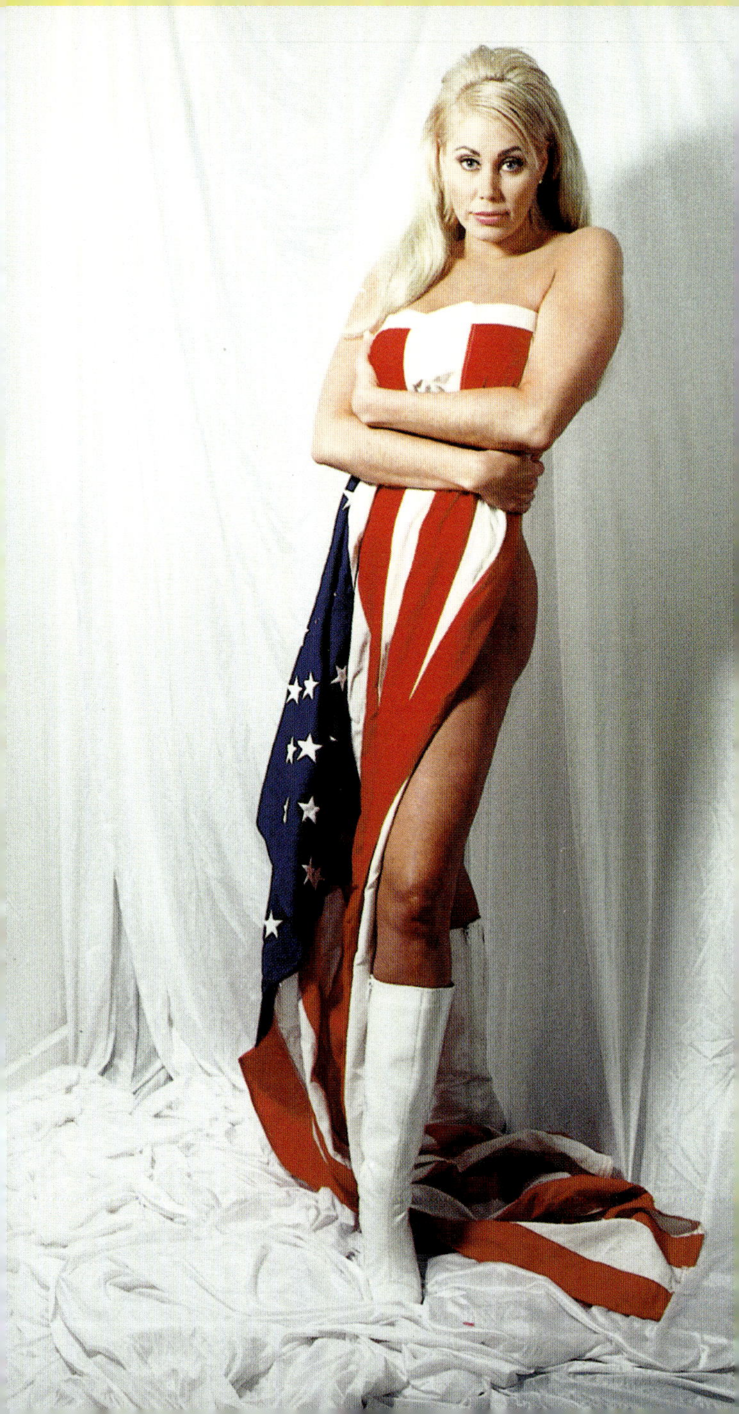

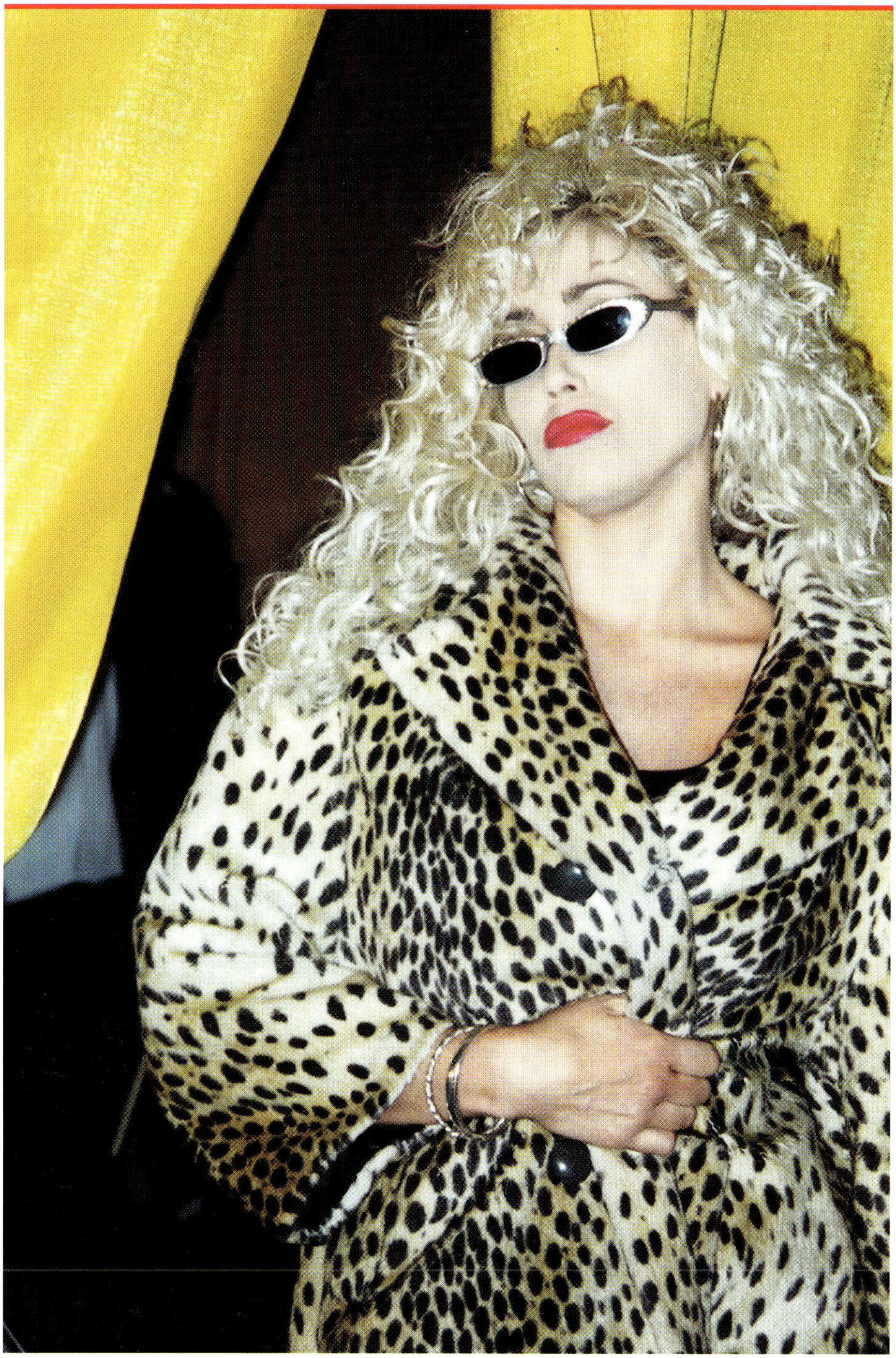

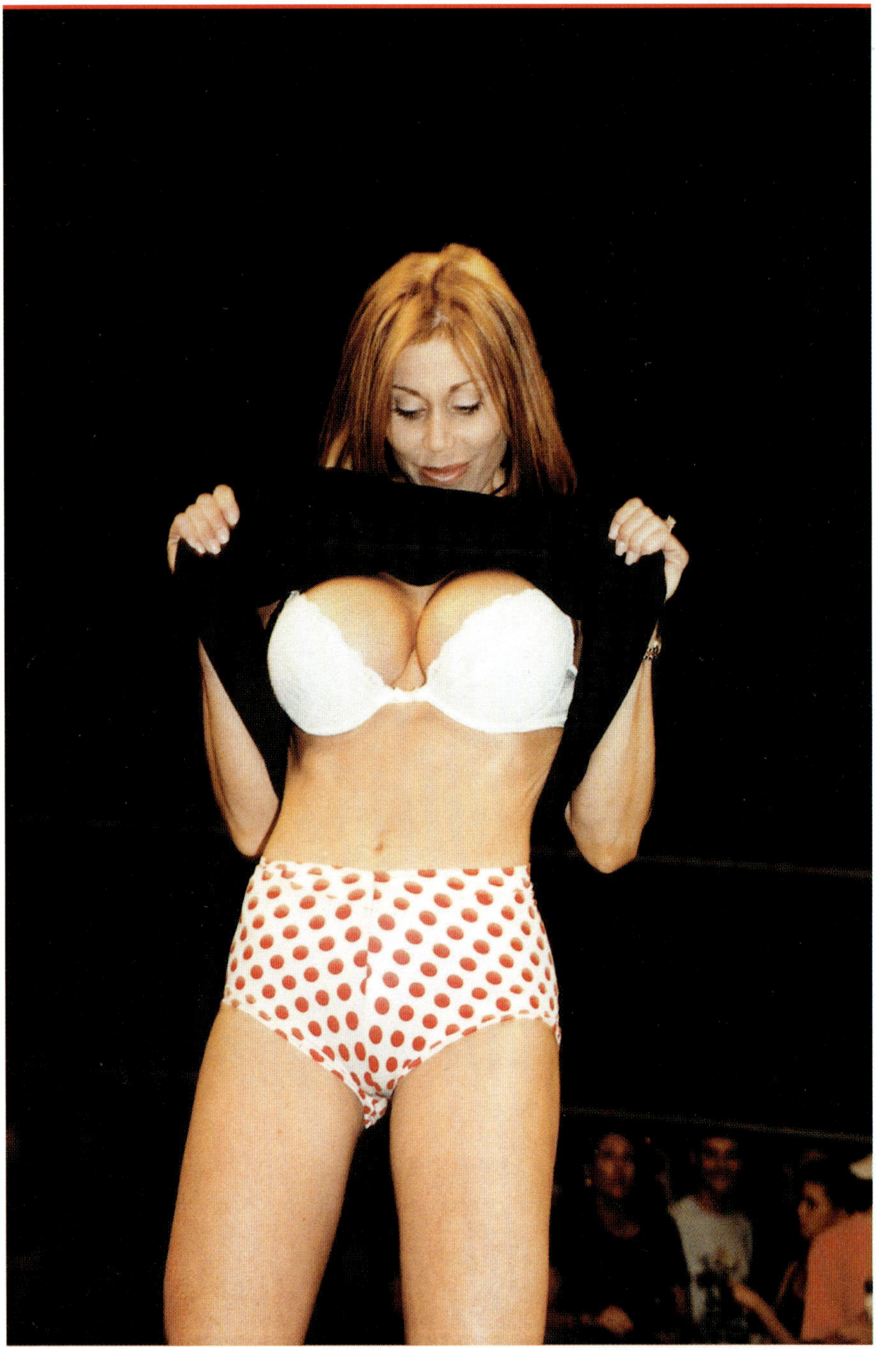

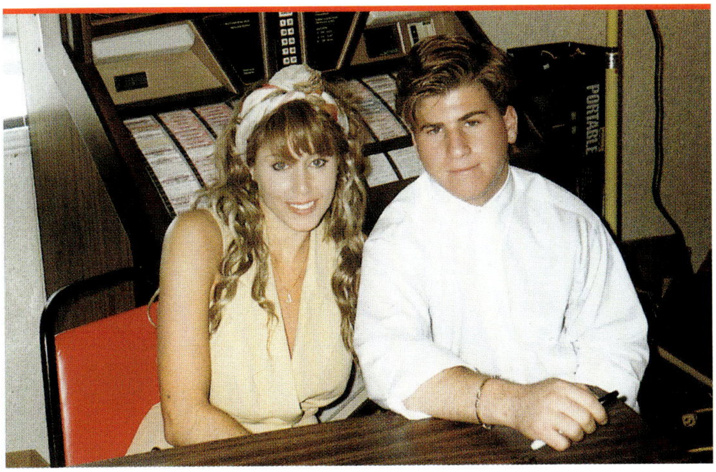
PORTABLE

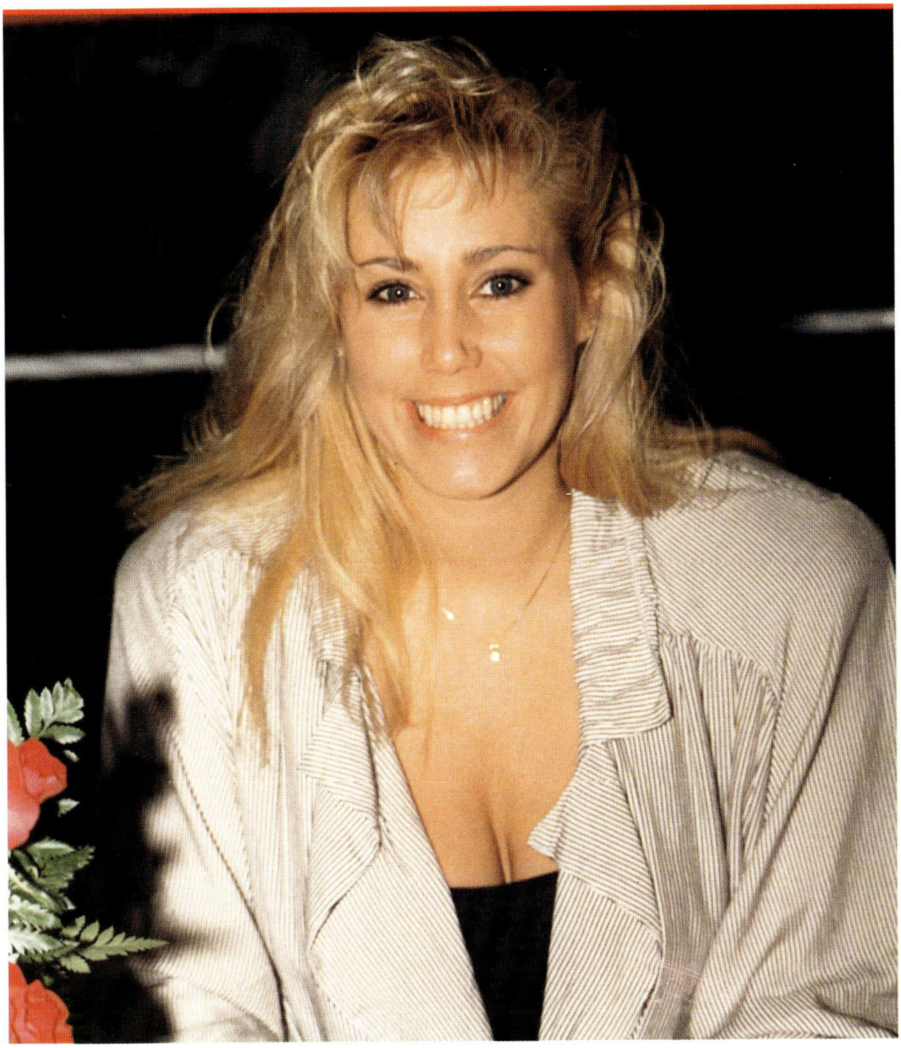

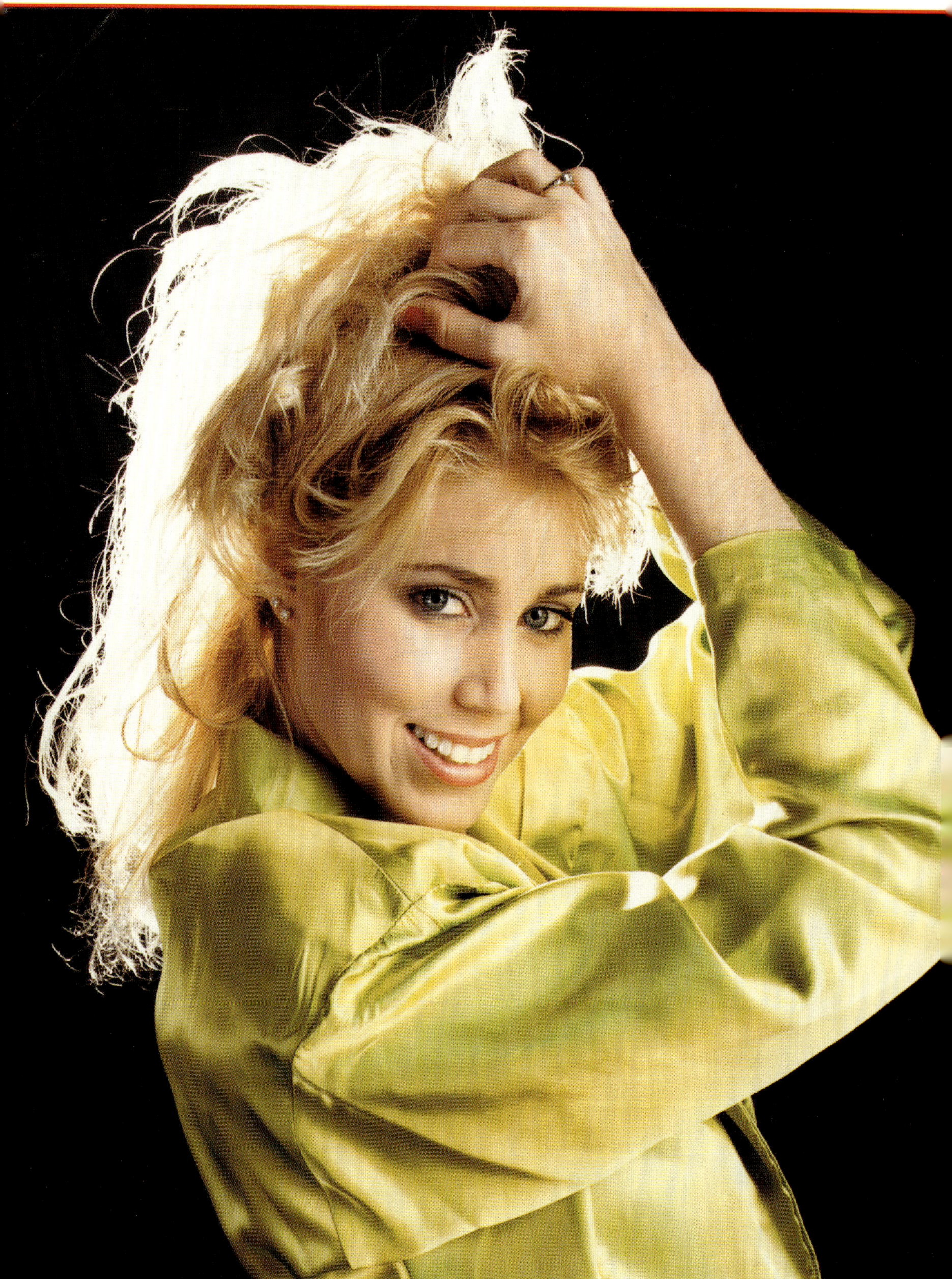

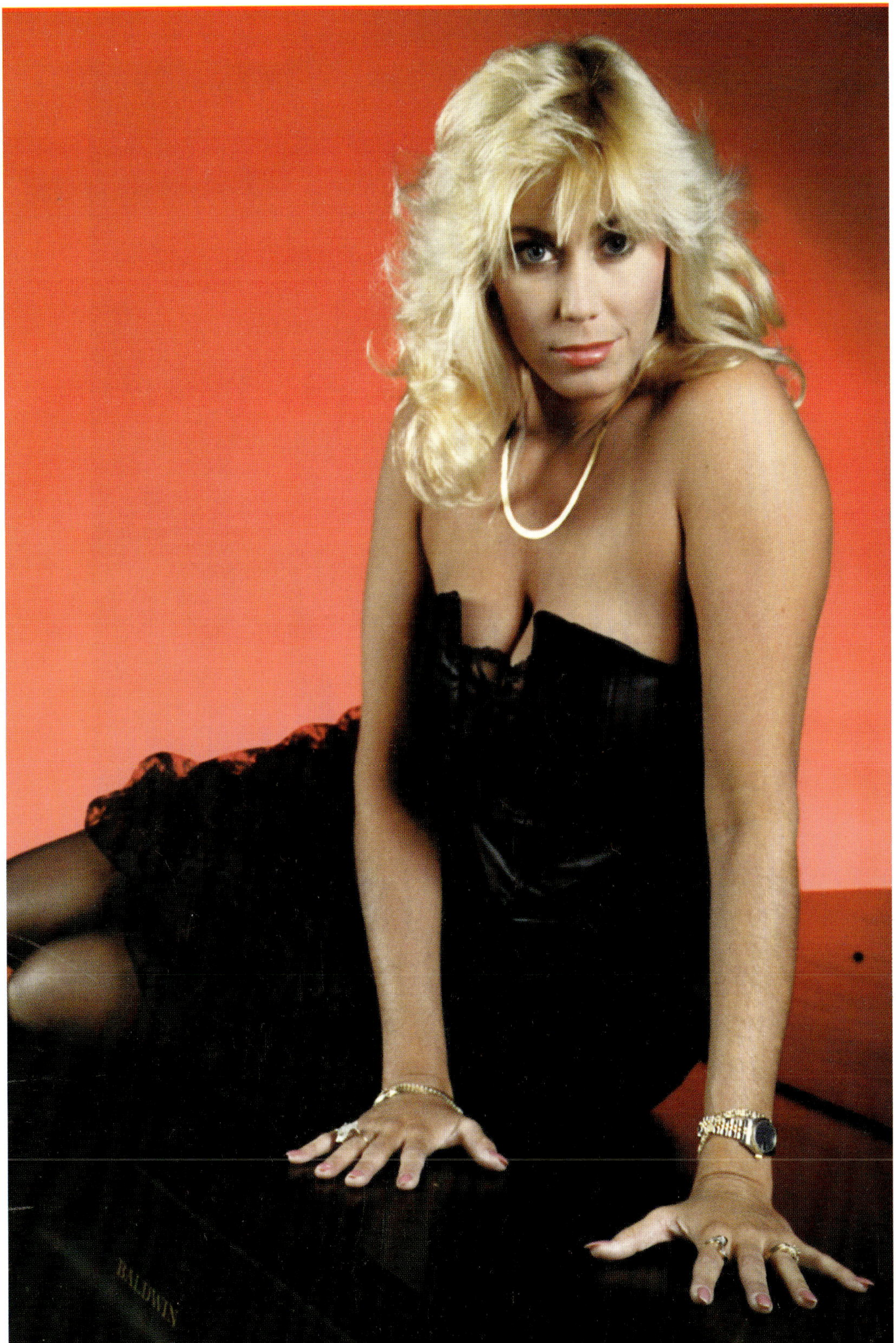
BALDWIN

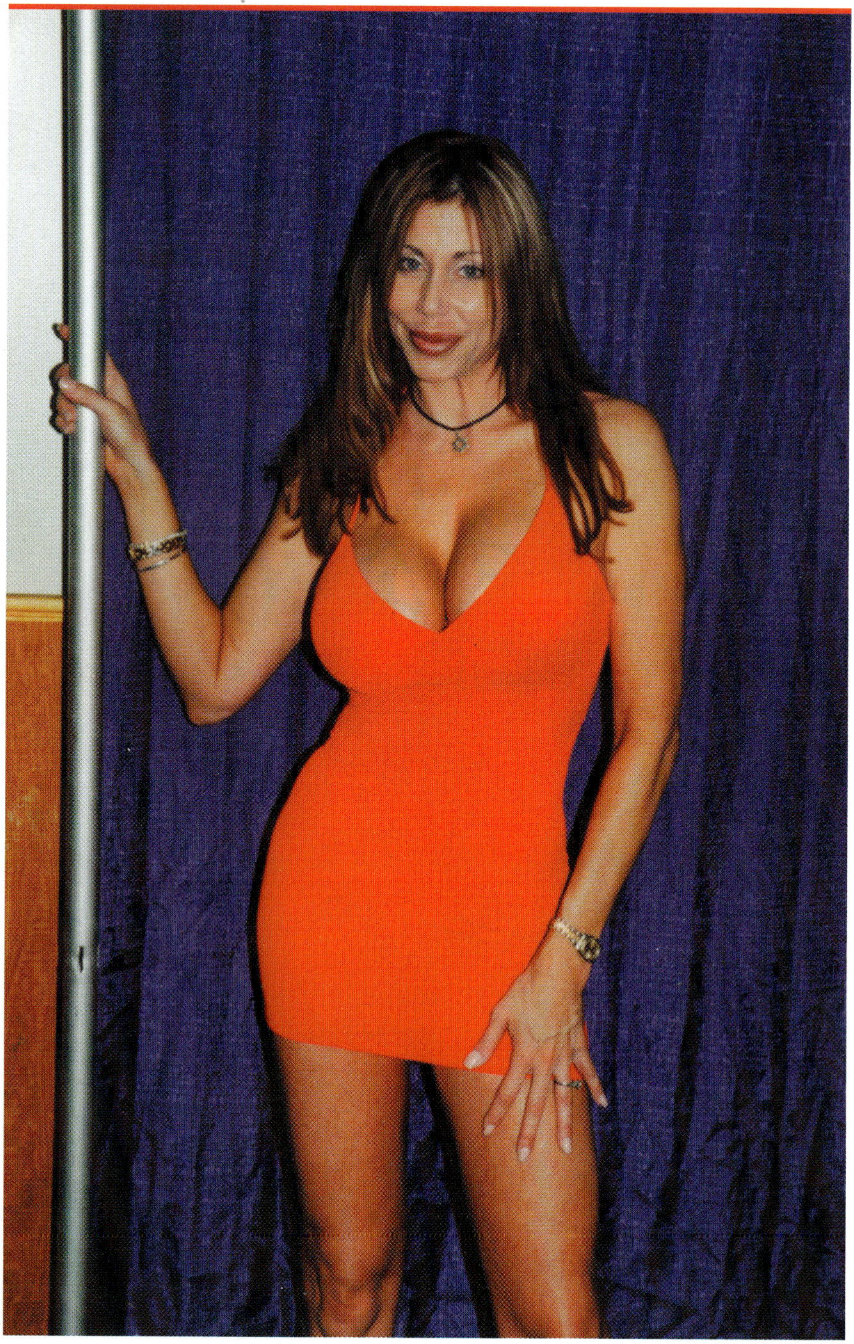

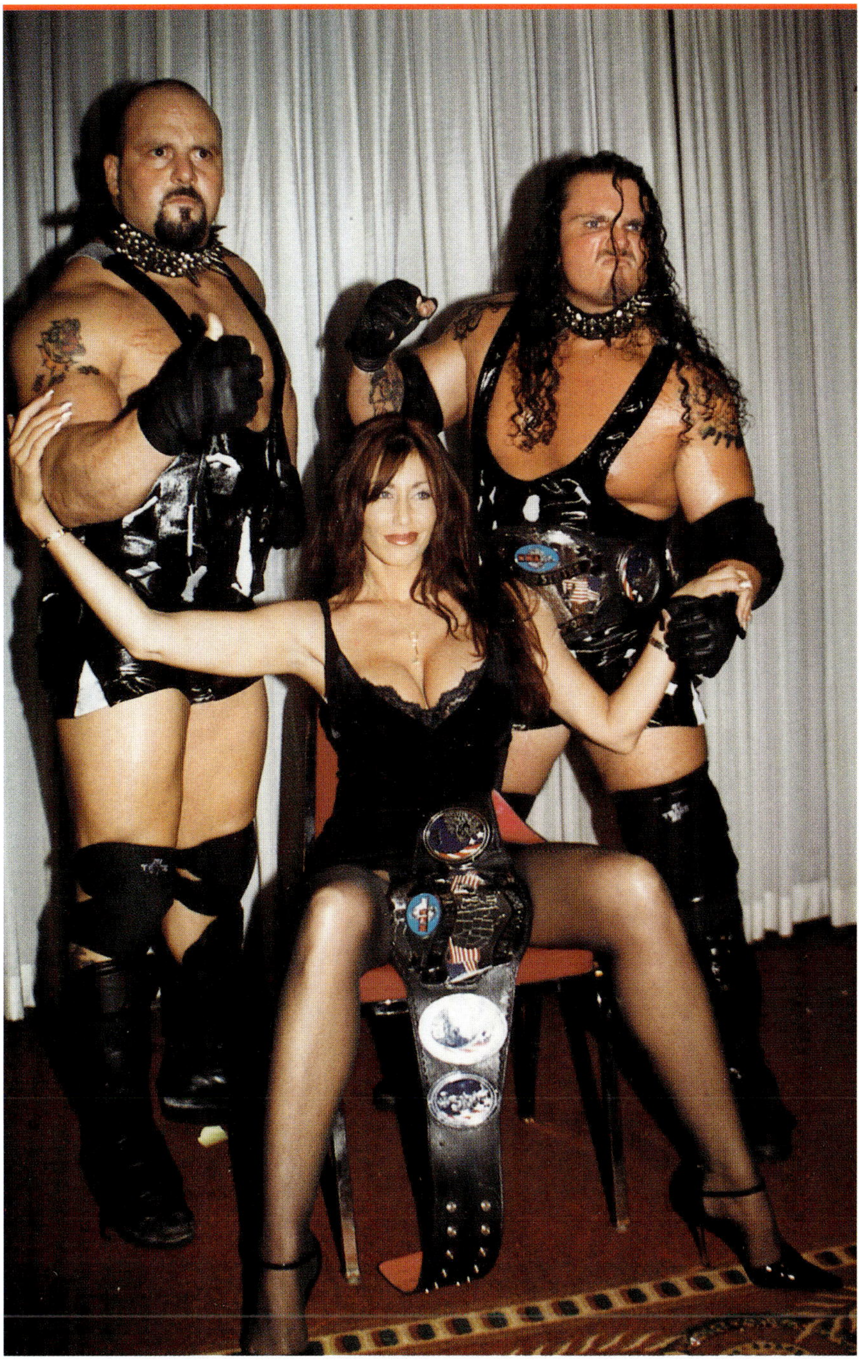

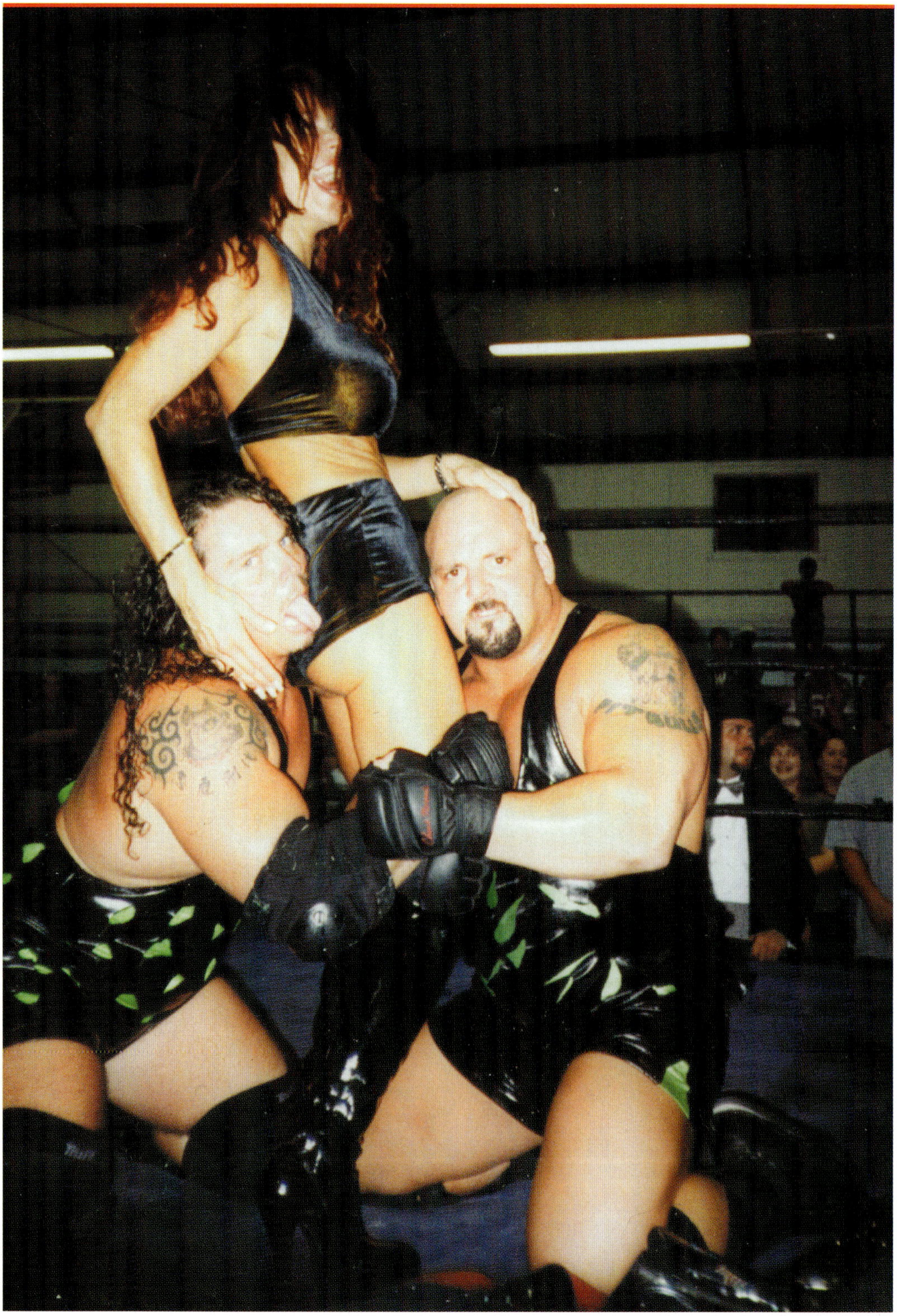

Missy Hyatt & Eddie Gilbert

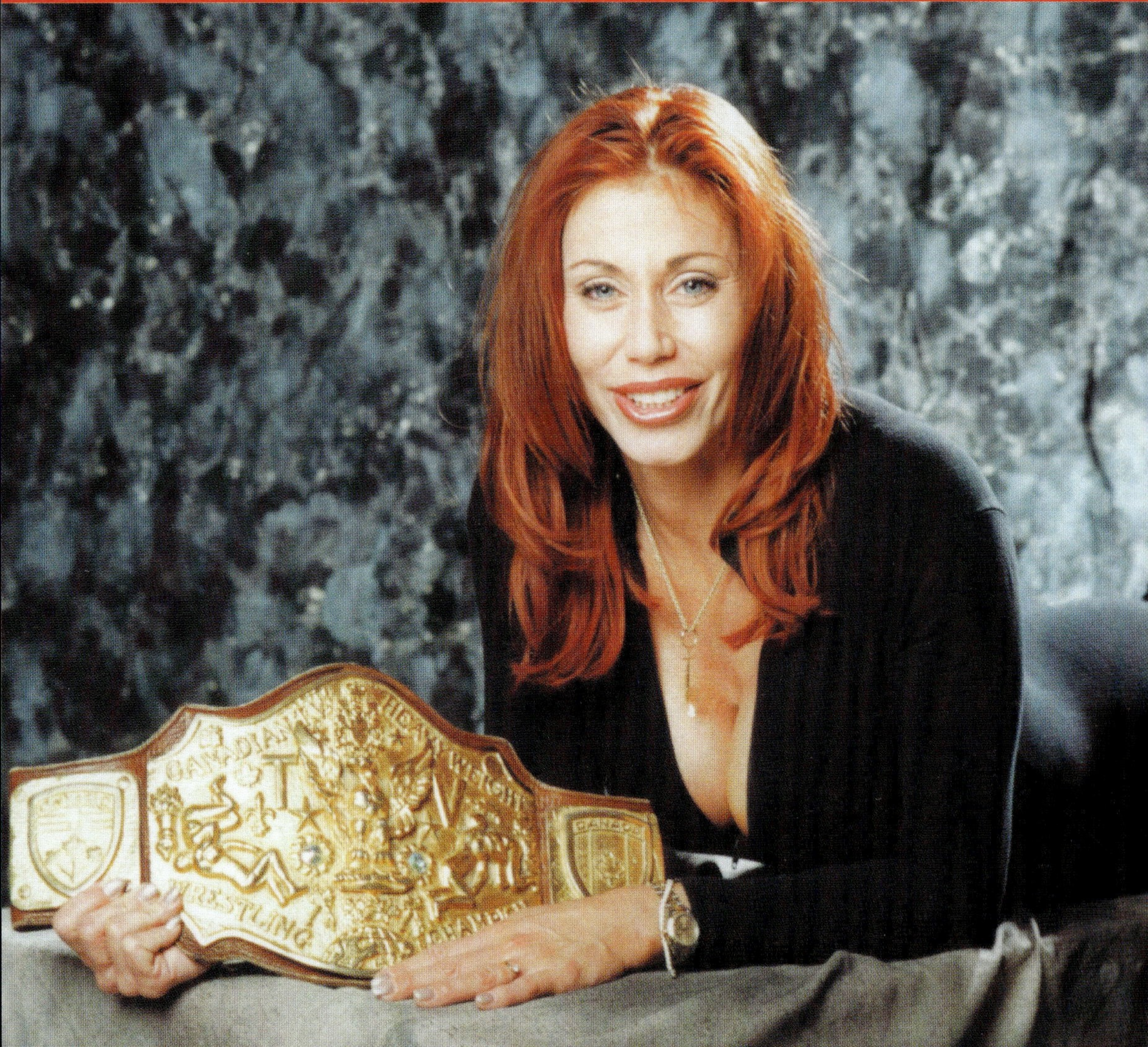
CANADIAN
WRESTLING

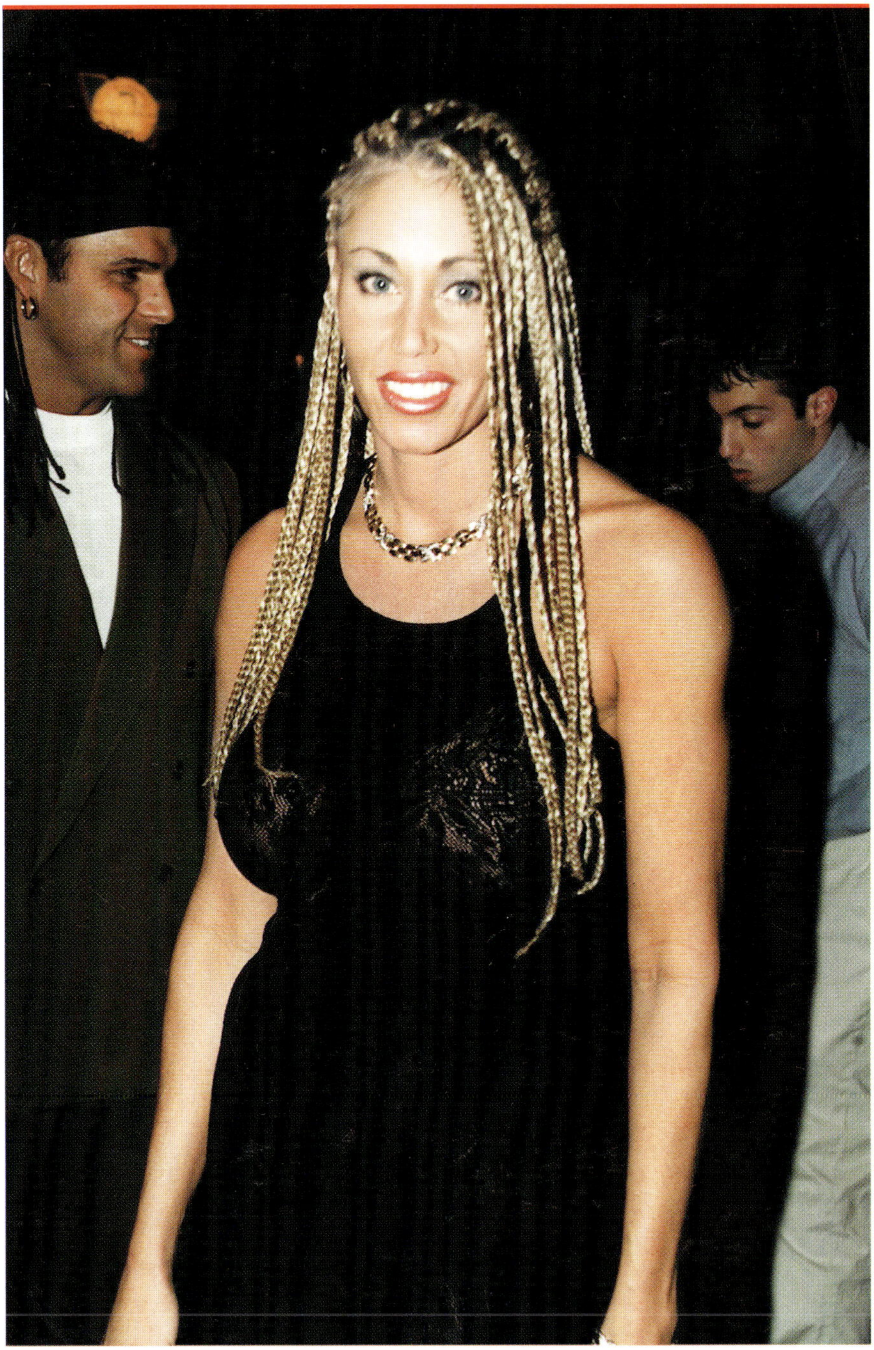

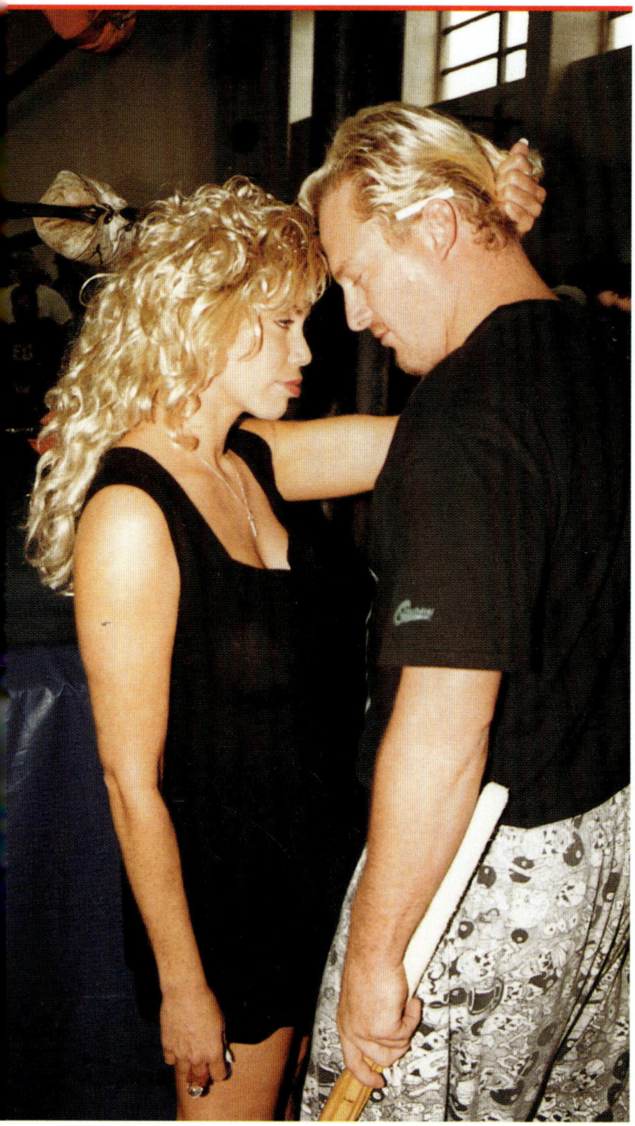

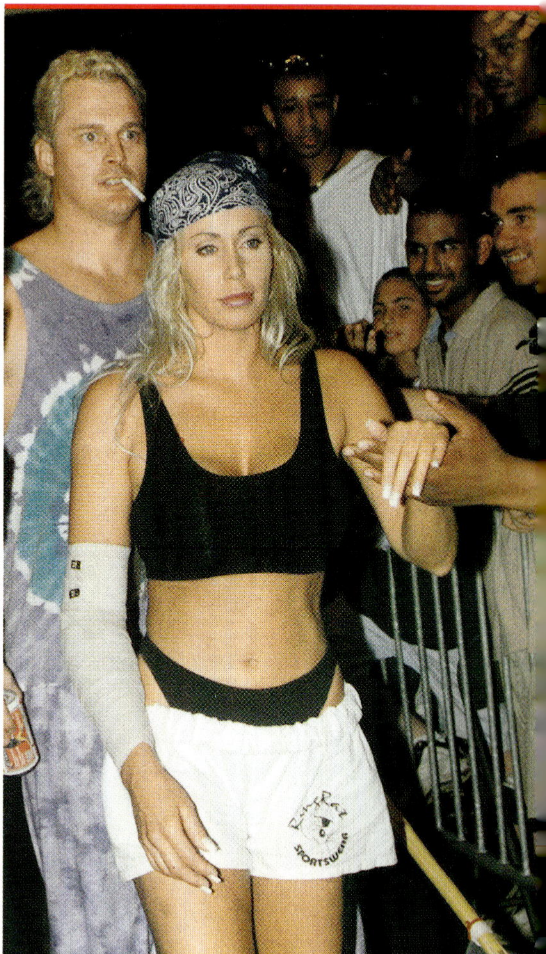
SPORTSWEAR

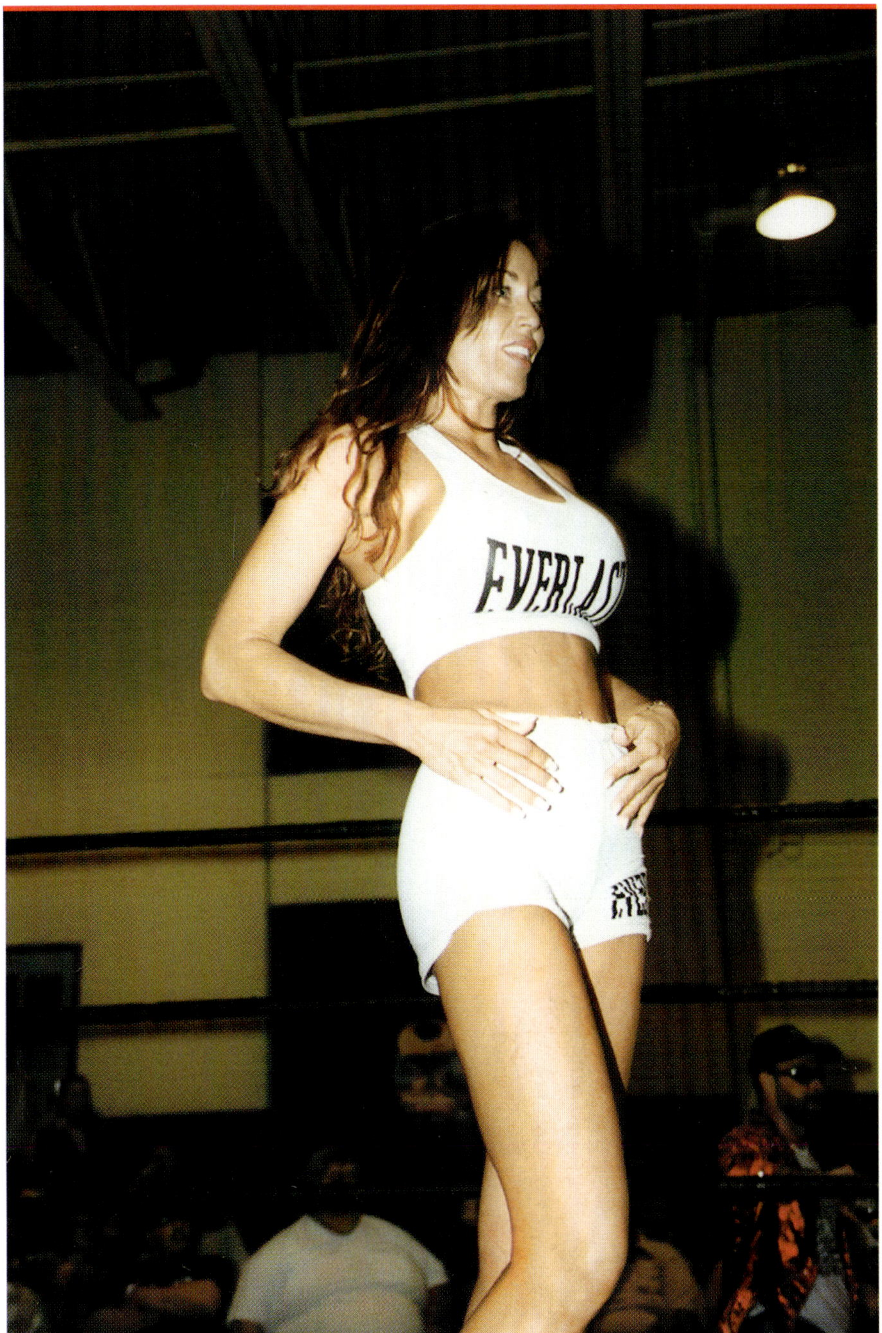
EVERLAST

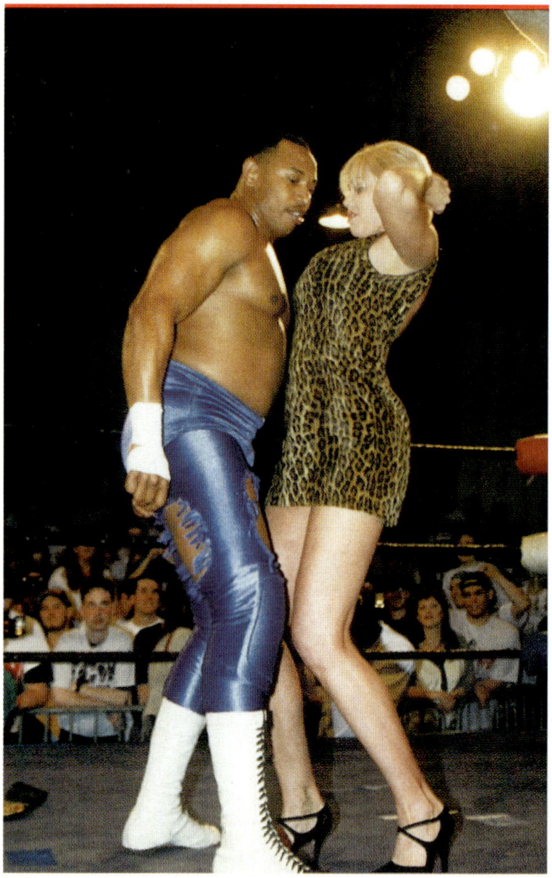

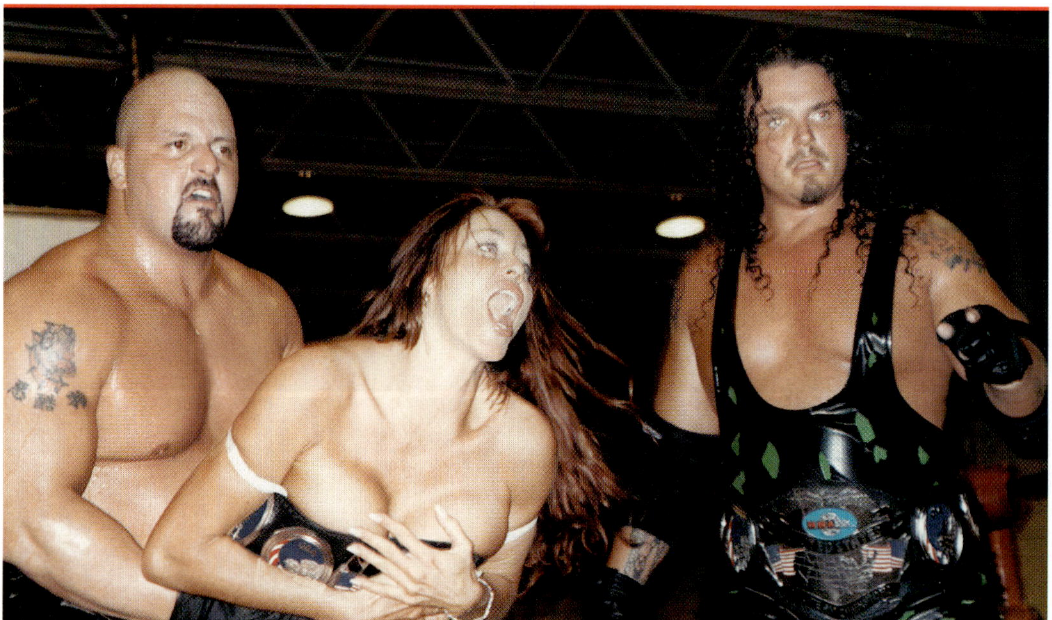

But of course Lawler kicks his ass, and Scotty slinks out of the arena without the date.

And that was the end of it — the angle, I mean. He went right back to being a jobber. Years afterwards, when he was wrestling main events as Raven with Extreme Championship Wrestling, Scotty and I used to laugh about that two-show angle. He thought he was getting a push, you know, thought he was going to wind up more than a jobber. He said to me, "Yeah, I got a push all right. I got a push right out of Tennessee!"

So Raven, Sid Vicious, Jeff Jarrett — those guys were just starting out. Except for Jerry Lawler himself, Eddie and I were the most recognizable names in the USWA, and the main reason we wound up there was Eddie's relationship with Lawler. Personally, I liked him a lot. He's one of the sweetest people in the business. The way he seems on television, you know, funny and sarcastic, that's how he is in person. But Eddie, he *worshipped* the guy. He grew up watching Lawler wrestle, and Eddie pattered his own combinations after Lawler's moves. He even wore the same kind of tights. In Eddie's eyes, Lawler could do no wrong.

To Eddie, he really was Jerry *the King* Lawler.

I remember once I asked Lawler if I could have one of his crowns to give to Eddie as a present. He didn't want to give it to me it at first — he never gave away his crowns. He's the King, so they were like his trademark. I mean, he had them specially made. That was the reason Eddie never bothered to ask for one himself. But I knew it would mean a lot to Eddie, so I asked . . . and asked . . . and asked, and finally Lawler coughed up a crown. I wrapped it up real quick and gave it to Eddie that night. At first, he didn't even believe it was a real Lawler crown; he thought I'd just had a copy made. But then, when I swore up and down it was the real thing, he was like a little kid, wearing it around the house. That crown became his pride and joy.

There's a sweet picture of Eddie holding that crown, beaming with pride. It's engraved on his headstone.

Eddie and I just about took over the USWA for the nine months we were there. Literally, I mean. We would show up for the live broadcasts Saturday morning, and we'd do interviews to open the show with the announcer, Lance Russell. Except after a couple of weeks of that routine, we began to move Lance Russell out of his chair and do the interviews ourselves. Eddie would interview me, and then I'd turn around and interview him — and poor Lance Russell would be left standing off camera, doing nothing. It became like a regular gimmick. Eddie and I would walk over to the interview area, and Lance Russell would look into the camera and mumble, "Oh, no, here we go again." And that would be the last the viewers would see of him for an hour.

Then, when that got old, we started bringing Eddie's family on air. For no reason, just for the hell of it. We brought in Eddie's dad to talk about his career as a wrestler. We even brought in Eddie's niece. She was nine years old, and she'd just won Little Miss Tennessee, so we brought her out in her crown and sash, and she twirled her baton, and then we interviewed her for fifteen minutes. I mean, it was *our* show.

Remember, this was *years* before the New World Order came along and started taking over WCW's broadcasts on TBS. I don't want to say they stole that idea from us. . . .

Well, yeah, actually I do.

※

Eventually, though, even the takeover routine got old. The USWA got old. Don't get me wrong. Jerry Lawler was great to us, gave us whatever we wanted, but the entire Memphis wrestling scene just got old real fast. What happened was, Lawler and his partner, Jerry Jarrett, would trade off every six months as head booker. Well, Lawler was the booker for our first six months in Memphis, and Eddie loved working with him, but then Jarrett came in, and he was bad news from the start. He wanted to bring in Michael Hayes and The Freebirds — which was fine. I mean, hey, if he thought he could afford them, more power to him. But he also wanted to shuffle things around to accommodate them, break up storylines that had been going on for months and script new angles that made no sense. What you have to understand is that Jerry Jarrett is . . . well, I guess I'll be polite and just say he's a piece of work. If there were a picture in the American Heritage Dictionary next to the word "redneck," it would be Jerry Jarrett. The guy keeps a cup on his desk and spits tobacco into it during business meetings.

No lie.

It was around the time Jarrett switched off with Lawler that Eddie got a phone call from David Woods, who operated the Continental Wrestling Federation in Montgomery, Alabama. Woods wanted to hire Eddie as the booker for the CWF. Not assistant booker. *Head* booker. Eddie jumped at the chance, and he was gone from the USWA within two weeks. I moved down to Montgomery with him, but I also agreed to pull double duty, to hang around in Memphis for another four weeks — it was like the least we owed Lawler — until we could figure out an angle that would lead to a big blow off.

So for four weeks I drove back and forth from Memphis to Montgomery. I announced the TV matches for the CWF. That was all I did in the CWF; Eddie didn't want me to manage anymore. He thought wrestling crowds were getting rowdier, and he figured I'd be safer as an announcer. But I was still managing in Memphis, in the USWA. With Eddie gone, I worked with Robert Fuller, the Tennessee Stud — who was just starting up a feud with Lawler. It was a natural for me because it followed up on Eddie's feud with Lawler. It was like the Stud was a hired gun Missy Hyatt brought in to take out The King.

Actually, I was the one who came up with an angle for the blow off. Lawler and the Stud would wrestle a one fall match — with the stipulation that if Lawler lost, he had to be my manservant for a day. But if the Stud lost, I had to be Lawler's maid for a day.

It wouldn't be right to mention Robert Fuller and not explain how he wound up with the nickname "Tennessee Stud." Well, the explanation is pretty basic. Robert Fuller has the biggest penis in wrestling. I never saw the thing myself, but I've heard lots of male wrestlers say they won't take their showers until he's done with his. I don't think it's envy. I think they're just afraid he'll turn around suddenly.

The only contender for that title, and again we're talking legend here, is Virgil. He swears he got his job with the WWF by pulling out his penis and laying it across the desk of a certain gay booker. Oh, and maybe Lanny Poffo — the Macho Man's brother. Rumor has it he could give himself head. But he was a contortionist, so it might be more a case of bending like Gumby than being hung like Pokey.

Which leads back to the USWA blow off. . . . Of course, Fuller loses to Lawler, and now I've got to be his maid for the day. And, of course, a camera crew rides out to his house to tape the whole thing. The crew is waiting in the morning when I show up in an evening gown at his front door. Lawler cracks open the door about three inches, but he won't let me in — he tells me I have to come in through the "servants' entrance" in the back.

The first thing Lawler makes me do is wash his car. He hands me a hose, but as he's handing it to me, he "accidentally" soaks my evening gown. And I'm yelling at him, calling him an idiot, telling them the bet's off because I didn't bring a change of clothes. So then he hands me, a Jerry the King Lawler tee shirt. And I'm like "Oh, no! No way am I wearing that! No way! The bet's off! I'm going home!"

Cut to the next scene: I'm wearing the tee shirt, vacuuming Lawler's living room floor. He's sitting on the sofa, watching me go back and forth with the vacuum cleaner. He's smiling, lifting his feet up whenever I pass. Then finally he says, "You know, that thing works a lot better if it's plugged in."

I slap my head and start over again.

Next, Lawler hands me a toothbrush.

"What's do you want me to do with that?"

"The kitchen floor."

The camera follows me into the kitchen, and now I'm down on my knees, scrubbing the tiles, bitching and moaning about how mean Jerry Lawler is, how he'll get his one day . . . and then, suddenly, you see these two muddy boots come stomping up next to me. Then I'm staring at the boots, and then down at the muddy footprints on the floor, and then you hear Lawler's voice, "I think you missed a spot."

The best part of the entire tape is the end. I've put in like seven hours and forty-five minutes of my eight hours, and I'm heading towards the front door, but then Lawler cuts me off. "All right, Missy, I've got one last job for you."

"What now?"

He hands me a long brush.

"Look," I say, "no way in hell am I scrubbing your back."

Lawler just smiles at me and points down the hall, towards the toilet. And I'm like, "Oh, *man*!"

So that's where the tape ends, with me on my hands and knees in the bathroom, scrubbing Jerry Lawler's toilet.

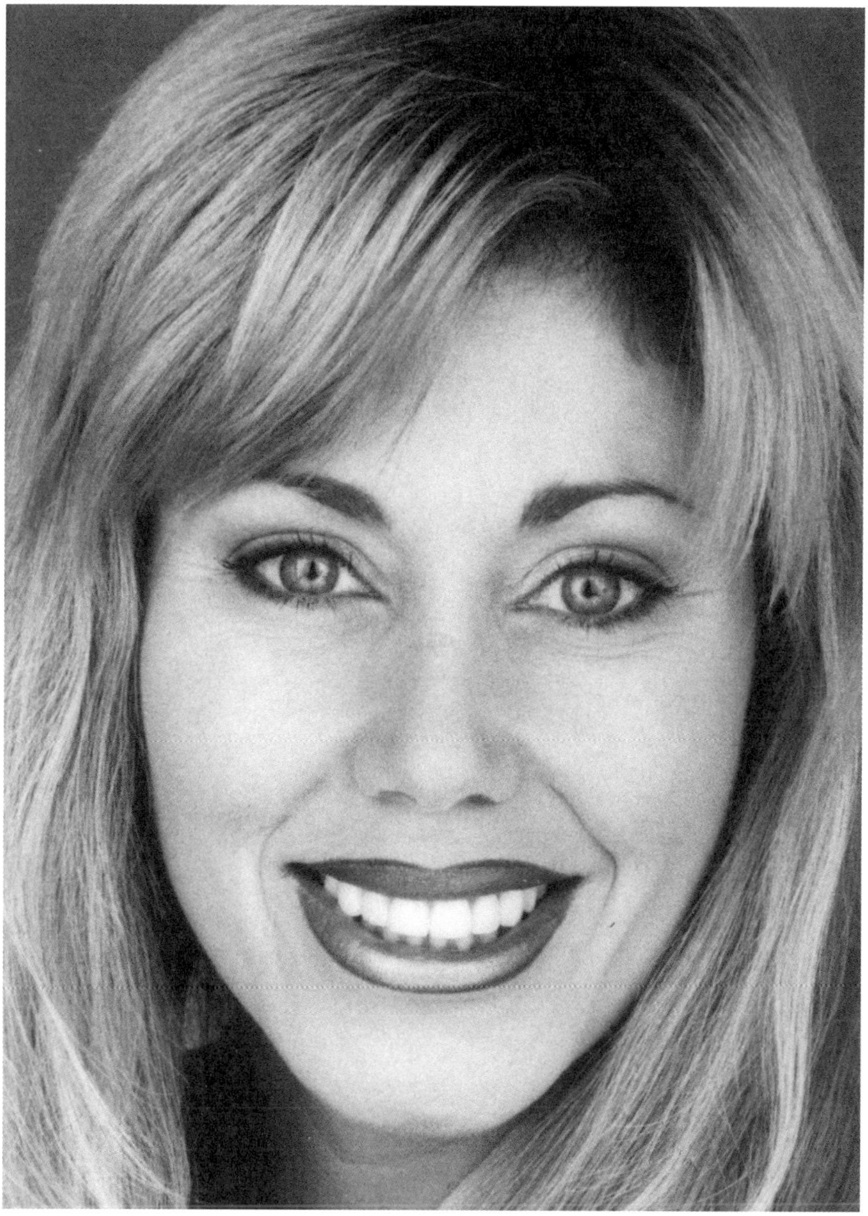

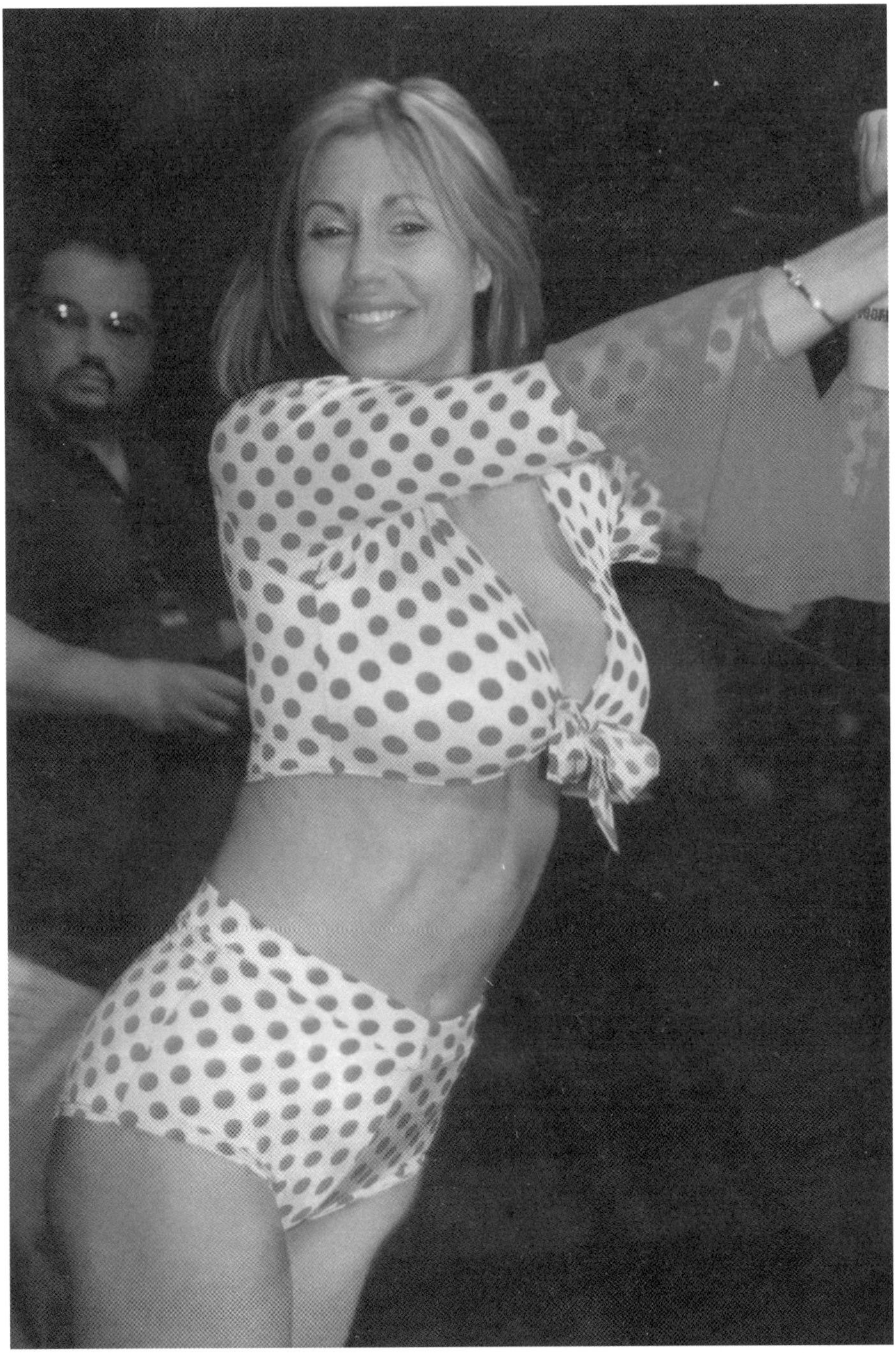

6

Alabama Getaway

Alabama, CWF

Eddie took the job with Dave Woods and the CWF because he wanted tpfo be head booker. But he also saw it as kind of the ultimate booking challenge. People in the business used to say that Eddie could take chicken shit and turn it into chicken salad; well, he was working with pure, unadulterated chicken shit in the CWF. I mean, talent-wise, he was working with guys who needed a yeast bath to rise from the bottom of the barrel. Guys who would've been jobbers in Memphis, which was not exactly prime time either, were wrestling main events.

The promotion, basically, was dying. Woods was losing money hand over fist. So he gave Eddie what he'd always dreamed about: a free hand. Whatever Eddie wanted to do, no matter how outrageous, Woods promised he wouldn't interfere.

The first thing Eddie did was bring in a young wrestler he'd scouted at Dominick DeNucci's camp up in Pittsburgh back when Eddie and I were still with the UWF. I remember him telling me about these two kids who were taking crazy bumps in front of like fifty people — they were flying off the top rope onto the concrete floor, diving head first into the metal stairs next to the ring. Insane stuff. Their names were Mick Foley and Troy Martin. Eddie got both of them try outs with the UWF. Martin eventually got a contract, but Foley didn't; he was kind of pot-bellied and round-shouldered, and Jim Crockett didn't think he had the right look.

Now, as it turned out, Mick Foley did just fine on his own. He went on to become Cactus Jack with WCW, and then Mankind with the WWF — and he wound up with a *New York Times* bestseller and as the most famous guy to lose an ear since freaking Vincent Van Gogh.

So when Eddie signed on with the CWF, he wanted to bring in Troy Martin — whose career with the UWF was going nowhere. Except neither of us liked the name Troy Martin. It just didn't do anything, you know? Well, Eddie and I were driving on some highway outside of Montgomery, and we spotted a sign for Troy, Alabama. That started us talking about Troy Martin, about how great a worker he was, and about how we had to come up with a better name for him. We started throwing out ideas, and I came up with "Douglas" — because I'd just seen the movie *Wall Street* with Michael Douglas. We both liked the sound of it, so then we were trying to figure out a last name that went with Douglas. Since I was already thinking about Wall Street, and since I had a crush on Charlie Sheen, I came up with "Douglas Sheen." That didn't work much better than Troy Martin. But "Sheen" started Eddie talking about the movie *Shane* because Troy Martin was blond and kind of looked like Alan Ladd.

About five seconds later, we shouted out at the same time: "Shane Douglas."

It's funny the directions people's careers take. The entire time he was wrestling with the CWF, Shane Douglas was also teaching part time at a junior high school. He used to work with rowdy kids. He was planning to go to graduate school, earn a master's degree and become a full-time teacher.

He almost did and could have wound up scribbling homework assignments on a blackboard in front of a classroom of pimply-faced kids, but instead he ended up signing autographs for pimply-faced kids, as The Franchise.

Now another guy who could've gone in a different direction, a *real* different direction, was the One-Two-Three Kid . . . also known as Six, also known as Six Pac, who eventually became X-Pac with the WWF. The first time I met him was when I started working in Montgomery. I was in New York City, doing an autograph signing and promoting the crap out of the CWF. He came up to the table where I was sitting, and he introduced himself; he told me he was going to a wrestling school up north, asked me for advice. I laughed and told him to get some steroids . . . I mean, the guy was a shrimp! What he didn't tell me, and what I found out many years later, was that he was a *major* party-er. The joke going around wrestling locker rooms back then was that "One-Two-Three" became "Six" to keep track of the times he'd been in rehab.

Hey, if it wasn't for wrestling, he could've wound up living in the gutter.

Like I said, Eddie didn't have much wrestling talent to work with in Alabama. He had Shane Douglas. He had Sid Vicious — who wore a mask and was still called Lord Humongous. He had himself. But he kept dreaming up unbelievable angles. I mean, he was serving chicken salad night after night. A big babyface in the organization was Pez Whatley, and one afternoon Eddie called Pez into his office and asked him if he'd be willing to work an angle with his 14 year old son — who was off from school. *No one* was doing family stuff at that point. Well, Pez talked it over with his son, and the kid was game, so the next week, during a television taping in Birmingham, the kid was sitting ringside for Pez's match with Eddie. In the middle of the match, Eddie's manager, Paul E. Dangerously, grabbed the kid out of his seat and started roughing him up, you know, shaking him by the shoulders. Then Eddie hopped out of the ring, and suddenly the two of them were slapping the kid around. I mean, the crowd almost rioted. They were surging up towards the ring, trying to protect the kid, trying to get their hands on Eddie and Paul E, cursing at them, hurling water and Gatorade bottles.

It scared the shit out of the kid. Not the angle. He was ready for that, but the crowd's reaction shook him up pretty bad. I remember going into the dressing room afterwards, and the kid was crying. Eddie felt real bad about it, but people were still talking about the incident weeks later.

Like I said, Paul E. Dangerously was working as Eddie's manager. I'll never forget the first time I met him. It was the week after Eddie signed on as booker. We were working a card in Atlanta, and we drove down from Tennessee.

I remember Eddie and I were standing outside a bar called Miss Kitty's in Marietta, Georgia, where the matches were being held, when a car screeches to a stop in front of us. This guy in a suit steps out of the driver's seat, and as he's stepping out of the car, he's talking on the telephone. Remember, this is 1989, so it's not like every Joe Blow has a cell phone. I step forward to shake his hand, but he waves me away. He's trying to finish the phone conversation. And I'm thinking, *Either this guy's putting me on or he's maybe the most obnoxious human being on the planet.* Finally, he yells goodbye into the phone and snaps it shut like it's a Star Trek fazer.

Then he turns to me and grabs my hand; I mean, he *grabs* it because it's just dangling at my side by now, and he says, "Paul E. Dangerously, glad to meet you." Next he turns to Eddie and says, "So how's the show going? Look, I've got a few suggestions . . ." And then he's off. He doesn't stop talking for the next hour. He's talking as the three of us turn and walk into the bar. He's talking as we're following the waitress to the table. He's talking as we're trying to decide what to order. He's talking about wrestling. About politics. About life. He was like a can of shaving cream, where you press down on the nozzle and this endless stream of *stuff* comes out. It didn't even sound like words after a while. Just a stream of stuff. Just sounds.

The thing was, after a couple of drinks, I started to like it. It was like a performance, like a gimmick. Except it wasn't a gimmick. It was Paul E. He was his own gimmick. He told us about the time he worked in Minnesota with Verne Gagne's promotion. Told us about how Gagne once flung the booking sheets in his face and said, "If you think you can book better than I can, here!" So Paul E. took the booking sheets from Gagne and started erasing stuff and writing in his own storylines. Then he handed the sheet back to Gagne a couple of days later, and Gagne could not believe that he actually did it, that he actually rewrote his booking sheets.

But just when Gagne was impressed with him, Paul E. walked out. He handed the book back to Verne Gagne and quit.

It was near two in the morning, and Paul E. was still talking. About how he could have been a lawyer because that's what his father was. About how he got his break in wrestling as a ringside photographer. About how he learned about survival growing up in the Bronx. (Actually, he's from Scarsdale, but Paul E.'s the kind of guy who'd rather climb a tree and lie than stand on the ground and tell the truth.)

On and on.

Finally, I reached across the table and put my hand over his mouth. His eyes got all crinkled, and I could feel him smiling against the palm of my hand. But the second I took my hand away, he was off again.

Eddie and I made it back to the hotel room at like four in the morning, and by now we're both dog-tired. He's beat from wrestling his match, and I'm beat from driving down from Memphis. So the two of us fall down on the bed, side by side, and just as our heads hit the pillows, the phone rings.

It was Paul E.

I fell asleep with the receiver against my ear.

Another guy Eddie brought to the CWF was Brother Earnest Angel. He wasn't a wrestler; he was a personality. He managed a few guys, but his main gimmick was dressing up like a Sunday morning preacher and goofing on Jimmy Swaggart. Brother Earnest was working in the USWA. Eddie brought him down to manage the Wild Samoans. He used to hold up a leather-bound videotape box which said "The Good Book" across it. He never used a real Bible; he never actually said the word God — he was real careful about that. But he would hold up the leather-bound videotape box, and then he would look straight into the camera and say, "With your help, I'm going to open up Wrestling Village, USA. It will be a sanctuary for wrestling fans nationwide. Open twenty-four hours a day, seven days a week, three-hundred-and-sixty-five days a year. Wrestling Village, USA. With your help, it will happen. Just put your hand on the TV screen. Can you *feel* it? *Feel* the power! If you can *feel* the power, send your contributions to me, Brother Earnest Angel, care of this station."

The punch line, of course, was that later on in the program he'd be managing one of his wrestlers ringside, and suddenly he'd crack open "The Good Book" and he'd have brass knuckles inside — which he'd toss to his guy, who'd use them to knock out his opponent.

Brother Earnest was like the greatest scammer I've ever met. He used to call up car services and talk himself in limo rides; it was uncanny. Like a gift from God. Week after week, the headliners would drive up to the matches in their own cars, and then Brother Earnest, who was really just a novelty act, would roll up in a stretch limo.

But one night in Birmingham, Brother Earnest outdid himself. That night's show ended a half hour late, so everyone was rushing to get changed and get out of the arena. Eddie had to finish his booking notes, so it always took him a little longer to dress after the matches. I remember walking out to the parking lot with Eddie and his brother, Doug — who was just starting out in the business. So the three of us figure we're the last ones to leave. But when we got to the parking lot, there was Brother Earnest, sitting on the hood of his usual stretch limo, motioning us to come over.

Brother Earnest calls out to us, "You folks heading back to Tennessee tonight?"

"Nah," Eddie answers him, "we're going to stay overnight and catch a flight back tomorrow morning."

Then Brother Earnest smiles at him, "C'mon with me. I can get you back tonight."

Well, we think it over for a minute, then climb in. It's the three of us in the back of the limo, plus Brother Earnest, plus our dogs Scooter and Sasha Girl. Yeah, it's a little cramped, but there's a wet bar, so we figure if the ride's on Brother Earnest, what the hell?

So we ride for about fifteen minutes, laughing and having a good time, and then, suddenly, the limo stops, and the driver comes around back and opens the door.

We're at the airport.

Now Brother Earnest starts smiling. "You ever flown on a Lear Jet?"

So I say, real sarcastic, "Why, you *got* a Lear Jet?"

Then he points behind us, towards the runway.

It's a Lear Jet.

So the four of us, plus the two dogs, rode from Birmingham, Alabama to Jackson, Tennessee in a Lear Jet.

The flight took twenty-seven minutes, runway to runway.

Brother Earnest's main tag team, like I said, was the Wild Samoans, two bushy-haired pot-bellied guys who were great workers but weren't supposed to do interviews . . . they were the *Wild* Samoans. Get it? So Brother Earnest became their mouthpiece.

Well, I'm interviewing them one time ringside, and Brother Earnest is going on and on about how they're going to squash whatever tag team gets in their way, and meanwhile the Samoans are grunting and nodding and looking mean. Then, suddenly, one of them reaches underneath the ring and pulls out a big red cooler. Brother Earnest glances down at the cooler, and then he looks back up at me and says, "Do you know what's in that cooler, lady?"

I have like no clue where he's going with this. I just shake my head.

"Open up that cooler for the lady. You see what's in that cooler? That's raw meat."

Now I'm like, "Oh, gross!"

But then one of the Samoans reaches into the cooler, pulls out a hunk of raw meat and starts chowing down on it.

"You see that, lady? That's what the rest of the tag teams are to us. Raw meat. They're just raw meat to the Wild Samoans."

Then the second Samoan reaches down into the cooler and pulls out a live lobster. I mean, the thing's claws are taped, and it's squirming around in the guy's hands.

I'm staring at the lobster, and then Brother Earnest leans in to the mike again. "And, lady, do you know what we're going to do to the rest of the tag teams in the CWF? Do you have any idea what we're going to do to them?"

Just then, the Samoan bites off the head of the lobster; I mean, I heard the thing squeal.

"We're going to eat them *alive!*"

The Samoan spits out the lobster head and flings the rest of the carcass onto the floor. Then the three of them, Brother Earnest and the two Samoans, storm off, like they've proved their point, and I'm left standing ringside, holding the mike, and I'm thinking, *God, this is such a skeezy job*. The fans in the front row, who heard the lobster squeal, are in shock. Except for a couple of boys, maybe twelve years old, who are sitting right behind me. They're imitating the noise the lobster made when the Samoan bit off its head.

Like, *Eee-eee*.

Then I hear the director's voice in my ear. "Go to commercial, Missy! Go to commercial."

So I look in the camera and say, "I guess that's all from down here."

Finally, the red light clicks off over the camera; we're in commercial.

As I'm about to head back to the announcer's table, though, I notice the lobster tail lying on the floor, ringside. And suddenly, without the head, it doesn't look so bad. I mean, I know how gross this sounds. But I was thinking, *Hmm, that kind of looks good.* So I kicked it under the ring, and then, after we finished taping, I found a plastic bag, and I took the thing home.

I had it for dinner that night.

Eddie was actually beginning to turn the CWF around, but then, out of the blue, he got a phone call from Dusty Rhodes who said that the UWF was long gone, folded into the NWA — but now Ted Turner was about to buy the entire organization from Jim Crockett . . . and change the name to World Championship Wrestling. The plan was to take on Vince McMahon and the WWF. Ted versus Vince. Ego versus ego. Eddie figured that meant big bucks. So he and I talked it over, and in the end, we decided to jump back to the NWA. I mean, there was no guarantee that Turner would offer us contracts once he took over.

It was a gamble, but we decided to go for it.

So we gave Dave Woods notice at the CWF — it's not like we were under contract, mind you; we were getting paid show by show, and the amount depended on gate receipts. Actually, Eddie was in charge of how much each wrestler got paid, and he always ended up shortchanging the two of us for the good of the boys. We were just scraping by. But Woods had given Eddie his break as head booker, so we agreed to stay on for like another month to work out our storylines.

Well, a couple of weeks later, Eddie was doing a show in Cleveland. I wasn't working that card, so I stayed home in Birmingham, packing our stuff, getting ready for the move to Georgia. When he returned the next morning, he told me he'd gotten ripped off: his diamond-studded wedding band and wallet, with a thousand dollars cash inside, had been stolen. He said he'd checked into a hotel after the matches, gone downstairs to the hotel bar for a bite to eat and left his stuff in his room. Then, when he came back a half hour afterwards, the ring and wallet were missing. He'd called the hotel manager, and the two of them had searched the entire bar, the lobby, even the elevators, but there was no sign of the ring or wallet.

The thing was, Eddie's story didn't add up. Wrestlers used to carry fanny packs for their valuables. Eddie had a Louis Vuitton pack, and I knew his routine with it. When he headed out of the dressing room to wrestle, he'd put his wallet, wedding band and Rolex watch in the fanny pack, and then he'd stash the fanny pack in his suitcase and lock it.

So if he'd gone back to the hotel and not taken the stuff out of the fanny pack, whoever stole his wallet and wedding band should have gotten his Rolex too — except there was the Rolex, still wrapped around his wrist. But if Eddie had taken the stuff out of the fanny pack before he left the arena, why would he have put on the Rolex and not the wedding band?

Plus, if he'd gone downstairs for a bite to eat, why would he have left his wallet back in the hotel room?

Suspicious, huh?

I was on the phone for hours the afternoon Eddie got back; I was calling up American Express, Visa, Mastercard, Sears, Walmart, K-Mart, Mobil, Texaco, Exxon, you know, canceling credit cards and ordering new ones. Not to mention the motor vehicle department. That call alone took about forty-five minutes. It was the biggest pain in my ass.

The entire time I was on the phone, a little voice in my head was nagging me, telling me something's not kosher about Eddie's story.

So after I got off the phone with motor vehicle department, I started calling wrestlers' wives and girlfriends. I figured maybe one of them had heard something about what happened in Cleveland the night before.

Well, no one knew about Cleveland, but I did find out that Lex Luger had been ripped off a month before. He'd met a woman in the hotel bar, and the woman had dosed his drink and then walked him up to his room. By the time they started to fool around, he was woozy. A minute later, he was out like a carp. She stole his stuff, and he never saw her again.

So I figured what happened in Cleveland was that Eddie checked into the hotel, slipped off his wedding band and left it on a nightstand, then headed down to the bar, picked up a chick and got doped out like Luger . . . but then, after she swiped his wallet and wedding band, she couldn't get the watch off his wrist. That made the most sense.

I didn't say a word about it to Eddie though, not for a week; I just kind of let it stew in my brain. Finally, though, I confronted him. He denied it up and down, got hysterical that I suspected him, but, really, he never did come up with an explanation that held together.

But what could I do?

I mean, we were about to move back to Georgia together. We'd given notice at the CWF. Dave Woods had already replaced us in Montgomery.

Plans were already in motion.

So I just didn't bother with it. I told Eddie I trusted him, which I didn't, and I let it pass.

It was a mistake.

If I'd pressed Eddie the rest of the afternoon, I'm sure he would've fessed up. He was like that. Guilt-ridden, I mean. Lots of people in wrestling have no sense of right and wrong; it's as if, when God was handing out consciences, they were standing in the wrong line. But Eddie wasn't like that. He used to keep me up at night, telling me how bad he felt that a wrestler wasn't getting the kind of push he'd been promised. Or even if he was getting the push but wasn't getting over with the fans, Eddie blamed himself.

Naturally, this situation was different — since it was his marriage, not his work. If I'd kept after him, though, I'm sure he would have cracked like a walnut.

But I let it pass.

Now what I've learned in therapy (I know what you're thinking: *Oh, God, she's going to talk about her therapy!* Well, tough titties! It's my book!) is that it's never a good idea to let stuff pass. Because you never *really* let it pass. Not if it matters. Then what happens is, like years later, you blow up — usually, at something trivial. Like your husband shushes you at the beginning of a movie. And then, suddenly, you're storming out of the theater, screaming back at him, "I know you French-kissed your secretary two years ago at the Christmas party!"

I only wish I'd blown up at Eddie in a movie theater.

What happened, though, was I cheated on him. It happened a month before we moved. Doctor Tom Pritchard was a major babyface who was in the middle of a feud with Dirty White Boy. And Dirty White Boy was managed by Dirty White Girl . . . which meant that he needed a woman to manage him.

So it was back to the catfights. I didn't mind though. I knew it was a short term proposition since everything was going to change as soon as Turner closed the deal.

The thing was, Doctor Tom was so gorgeous. He had long, curly brown hair, a cut body, and a soft voice. And he was real nice to me.

Especially in the ring. Dirty White Girl wasn't bad to work with, but she was a little green, and Doctor Tom was always careful to pull us apart whenever it looked like she was getting carried away.

Plus, I was still pissed at Eddie for what happened in Cincinnati.

You can guess what happened next. It was after a show in Vicksburg, Mississippi. Dr. Tom and I had been like "accidentally" rubbing against each other the entire night. Passing one another in the dressing room. Huddling before the match. Walking to the ring. Neither of us said a word about what was going on. But it was like our bodies were carrying on a discussion — you know, the way bodies do when things between them are about to turn physical.

So after the matches, we walked out to the parking lot together. Our cars were parked side by side. I opened my car door, and he opened up his, and then he said something like, "See you later, baby," . . . and then suddenly we both turned around and lunged together. I remember slamming my car door shut with my foot as we were kissing.

Maybe a second later, we tumbled backwards into the front seat of his car. We were like a couple of high school kids. Lots of kissing and groping. I mean, we were still wearing our clothes. My blouse was wide open, and my boobs were hanging out of my bra; I had my hand down the front of his jeans. And it's real sweaty, about 100 degrees in the car, about 85 outside, and the windows are fogging up, and the car's rocking back and forth, and meanwhile wrestlers and fans are walking by us on the way to their cars.

By the next morning, the entire organization knew what had happened.

Which meant Eddie knew.

But of course he never said a word about it. The two of us just kind of stormed around the new house pissed at one another. I knew that he knew about Dr. Tom; he knew that I knew about Cleveland. It was like we were sitting on an emotional bomb, and neither of us had the strength to light the fuse.

Steiner Brothers

7

Ted and Missy's Bogus Journey

Georgia, WCW

After a couple of months, Ted Turner's WCW closed the deal to buy out Jim Crockett, and then Jim Ross turned around and offered me and Eddie contracts for two years. I started out managing Eddie and Rick Steiner, then Rick's brother Scott came along, and it was the four of us — the Steiner Brothers, Eddie and me. There was talk about resurrecting the Hot Stuff and Hyatt International angle, but Eddie decided it was played out.

I think, maybe, in his heart of hearts, he sensed what was coming.

Eddie also wound up on Turner's booking committee. I mean, it really was a *committee*. Very corporate. The entire committee wore suits — in fact, we used to call them The Suits. There was Eddie. Dusty Rhodes. Ric Flair, Kevin Sullivan. Jim Ross. Oh, and a businessman named Jim Herd who used to run a string of Pizza Huts. What his connection was with wrestling, I never did figure out.

But Eddie was into it, I mean, the entire corporate image. He went out and bought a new wardrobe. Armani suits. Ralph Lauren suits. Brooks Brother shirts and ties. Two hundred dollar shoes. He would head over to the CNN Center in Atlanta in his suits, looking *so* handsome, and he'd come home and tell me about the latest pep talk Dusty gave the committee, about how he expected them to kick Vince McMahon's ass.

But right off, there was trouble. Kevin Sullivan hated Eddie. Why he

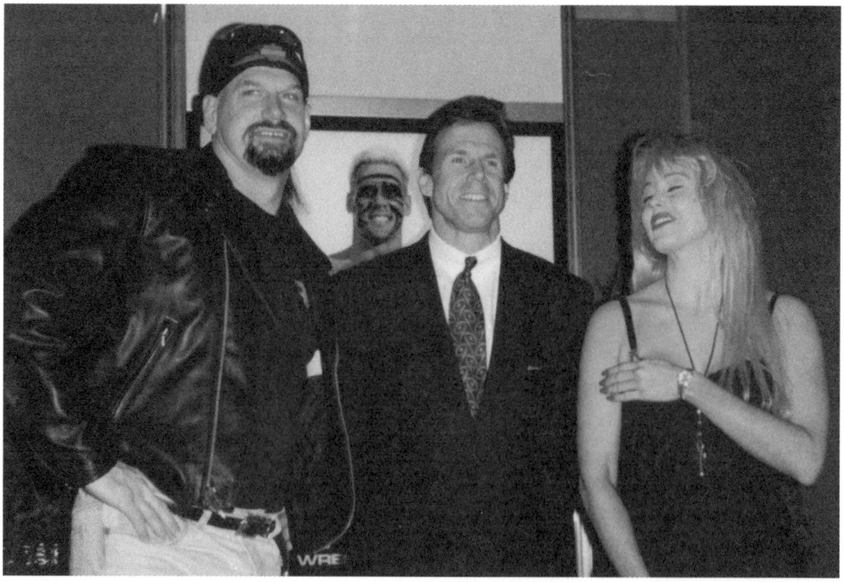

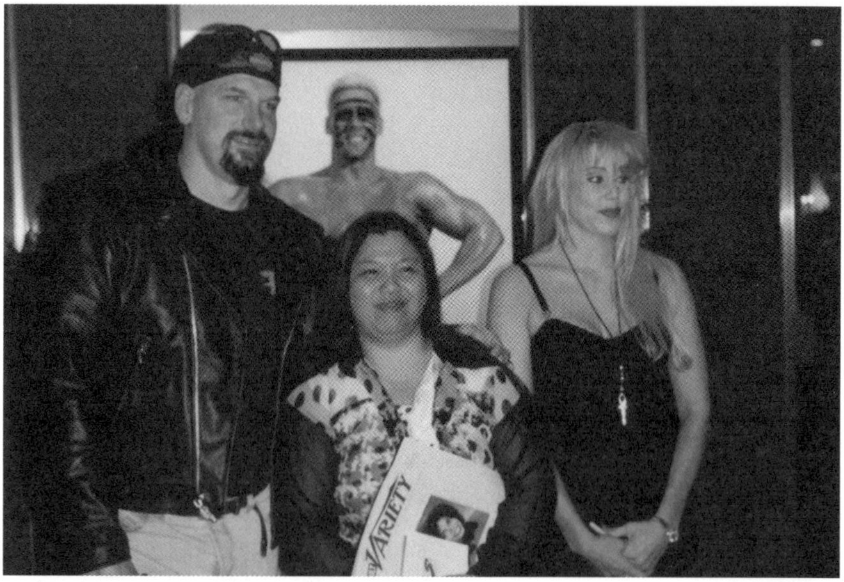
VARIETY

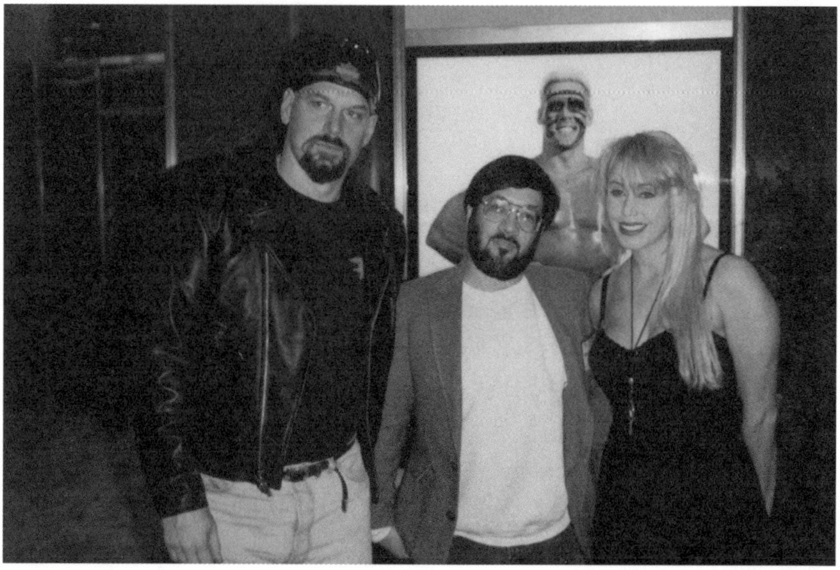

*Schmoozing with
the future guv*

hated Eddie is a mystery — maybe because their backgrounds were so alike. Both came along around the same time as bookers, both also managed and wrestled, both eventually brought in their wives to work angles with them. But you could just as well say those are reasons they should've become friends. Maybe Sullivan hated Eddie because the two of them worked the same way, but Eddie was flat out more successful.

Who knows?

Hey, maybe it was because Kevin Sullivan worshipped the devil.

And, *no*, I'm not kidding.

Whatever the reason, from their first week together on the booking committee, Sullivan started backstabbing Eddie. He'd wait for Eddie to leave the meetings, and then he'd run around to the rest of the committee and convince them to shoot down Eddie's ideas. (I found this out years later from Dusty Rhodes and Jim Ross, and also Nancy, Kevin Sullivan's wife . . . who later became "Woman" . . . who later became Kevin Sullivan's ex-wife.) And Eddie would come home from work, and he'd be miserable. He'd sit up in bed half the night, wondering why all his ideas were getting shot down. I'd wake up at three in the morning, and he'd still be awake, muttering to himself, "I *know* I can book this stuff."

I don't want to say too much about Kevin Sullivan — it's like a waste of trees even to spend a single page on him. So I'll just say this. I ran into Nancy Sullivan in 1999 at the Brian Pillman Memorial Show. Now keep in mind that Nancy and I spoke about ten words to one another during the entire time she was with WCW. That's saying a lot since we worked a long angle together when I was managing the Steiner brothers.

So I ran into her backstage at the Pillman Show, and she looked beautiful. I knew she'd left Sullivan a year before, and now she was with Chris Benoit, and I kind of waved to her, and then she came over to me and said hello . . . and then, for the first time, we sat down and talked. I told her how good she looked, and she said, "Yeah, I got away from Kevin."

So I said, "The day that man dies, I'm dancing on his grave."

Then she said, "Well, that's going to be a long conga line."

I'll never forget the first time I met Ted Turner. It was at Center Stage Arena in Atlanta. He came down from his offices at CNN Center to take promotional photos with Ric Flair and a few of the other main guys, and then he took a tour of the arena. He must have asked to meet me too; people were already pointing towards me, you know, like, *She's just over there!* when I spotted him. Naturally, I rushed over to introduce myself.

He was shaking hands left and right — publicists, maintenance workers, camera operators. But as soon as he saw me coming, he waved them aside. He took two steps towards me, and then we came together; he put out his hand, and I put out mine, but then he reached past my hand and slipped his arm around my waist. It was a real slick move. He slid in real close, pressing his side up against my boobs. He was wearing like a cheap-ass J.C. Penny suit. And I could smell the bourbon on his breath, either bourbon or scotch. As he snuggled up even closer, he whispered in my ear, "Hey, baby, want to mud wrestle?"

Then he grabbed my ass.

Now of course this happened before he was with Jane Fonda. But it still creeped me out. I mean, I walked away thinking, *What a cheap ass redneck!*

Ric Flair was another person who creeped me out on a regular basis. Though to give credit where credit is due, the man's got a gift. I don't mean his wrestling; I always thought he was the hammiest worker going. His *real* gift is that he can talk just about any woman out of her clothes . . . in public! I can't count the number of times a group of us stopped by a bar, and he pointed to a chick sitting by herself and said, "A hundred bucks I can get her naked in an hour." Mind you, he'd always pick the woman who looked least like the type, you know, like the geekiest English teacher. Then he'd saunter over, introduce himself, and start ordering Kamikazes — that's what he's known for, Kamikazes. The next thing you know, the chick's up on a table, her bra's hanging from the overhead fan, her skirt's up over her head, and she's going crazy. I think his proudest moment wasn't any of his fourteen world championships — or whatever

Here's me with Ted Turner — before Jane

number he's up to now. It was one night in Bennigan's in Atlanta when he got three flight attendants to take off their clothes and dance on the bar.

Let me tell you something about Ric Flair. The guy's a perv. We're talking Marv Albert City here. First of all, he's got a thing about pubic hair. He loves it. He won't have sex with a woman who shaves. His saying used to be, "No hair, no Flair." Flair's main thing, though, was that he always wanted to show women his penis. Publicists. Make-up and wardrobe people. Waitresses. Department store clerks. Travel agents. Bank tellers. I mean, it wasn't even so much a sex thing. It was a perv thing. He just liked showing off his penis — though, frankly, I've seen it dozens of times, and it's nothing to write home about. I mean, basically, it just looks like Ric Flair's penis, like the kind of penis he would have. Put a bleached-blond wig on it, and it would look like him.

Whoooo!

Before we leave the subject of penises — again! — I guess I should mention the Lex Luger Game. It was something Bonnie Blackstone and I invented. It was like the Bob Newhart Game — you know, where every time a character on the old Newhart show says "Bob," you down a shot. Except instead of "Bob," we used Luger's penis. You see, Luger is always touching himself when he wrestles. Sometimes, he just brushes his hand across his groin, you know, just checking to make sure everybody's hanging right, but sometimes it's as if he's working his balls like a freaking abacus. So Bonnie and I invented a drinking game. Every time Luger grabbed himself, we took another shot.

We had to stop after a couple of times though because we wound up under the table.

By April of 1989, Eddie and I were going through major marriage problems. He was miserable, personally. His storylines were still getting shot

No hair, no Flair!

down left and right by the booking committee — even the angles he came up with for himself. I remember one week he came home convinced he was about to become one of the Four Horsemen. He was sure it was going to happen because Dusty had given him his word. But then it fell through. I'm sure it was Kevin Sullivan, backstabbing him as usual, but this one hurt a lot because being one of the Four Horsemen was always of dream of Eddie's. He laid in bed an entire weekend after that, just watching television. He didn't eat. He didn't shower. He just lay in bed and yelled at me whenever I tried to talk to him.

Naturally, after what happened in the parking lot with me and Dr. Tom, pretty much everyone in the business knew our marriage was shot to hell. I mean, Eddie was never the kind of person who could hide his emotions anyway. So now people would see him moping around, and they'd shoot him real sympathetic looks, you know, like, *Poor guy!* Which of course he despised. Then he'd come home, and he'd blame me for making him a laughingstock — though, of course, he'd never mention the incident with Dr. Tom. Instead, he'd accuse me of talking about our problems behind his back.

Finally, at the end of the summer of 1989, Eddie decided to leave. Leave WCW. Leave our house in Kennesaw. Leave me. The thing was, he just picked up and left. There was no big scene. No yelling. No tears. I was sitting at the kitchen table one night, reading the newspaper, when he came home. I heard his key in the lock, but I just kept on reading the paper. He walked into the kitchen, kissed me on the forehead and said in a soft voice, "Baby, I got to get out of here. I'm losing my mind."

By the end of the week, Eddie was out of his WCW contract, and he was gone.

He took Scooter. I kept Sasha Girl.

※

The house in Kennesaw was too big for me, alone, so I started to look for an apartment in Atlanta. The third afternoon, the real estate agent was showing me an apartment complex ten minutes from my old house. As we walked through the front gates, I noticed this good-looking guy in cut-offs and a muscle-shirt washing his car. I mean, this guy was *hot*. Dark tan. Ripped stomach. Plus, it's a warm day, so he's like glistening with sweat.

I turn to the agent and say to her, "I don't know what apartment is next to his, but that's the one I want."

She nods her head and says, "Oh, that's a one bedroom with a den. It's got a big Jacuzzi tub. You'll love it."

I look at the apartment, but it's like a formality at that point because I know I'm going to take it, and then I write out a check for the month's deposit. Then I kind of shoo the agent away so I can introduce myself to the hot guy washing his car.

He's still at it when I come back downstairs.

"Hey there," I say, walking over to him. "Looks like we're going to be neighbors. I'm Missy. Missy Hyatt."

He starts smiling. "Yeah, I know you. You're in wrestling."

So I'm like, "Guilty!"

"Well, I'm Mark. Mark Bagwell."

"You watch wrestling?"

"All the time, honey. All the time."

"You ever think about getting into it?" I ask. "You've got the look."

He kind of blushes. "You think?"

"Yeah, you're big enough. Buff enough, I mean. *Real* buff."

Nowadays, you know that guy as Buff Bagwell. And let me tell you, Buff is the stuff.

I moved into the apartment next to Buff Bagwell, but it turned out that he already had a girlfriend, and the entire complex had thin walls, so I wound up listening to Buff do his stuff five nights a week. Meanwhile, I was still getting accustomed to the idea that I was on my own — I mean, I hadn't been alone for more than a couple of weeks since before I dated Jake Roberts. Now, suddenly, when I woke up in the morning, it was just me.

For the entire day, it was just me.

I hated it.

Yeah, I know, it's *uncool* to admit that. But I like having a man around. I've always gotten along better with men than with women. It's not even the sex, or at least it's not *just* the sex. It's more like, I *understand* men. I know what to expect from them. I know how they think, what they want . . . and how they think they're going to get what they want. Men make sense to me. Women are too complicated. Men are basic arithmetic, and women are calculus. I mean, who wants to take calculus unless you're getting four credits for it?

So I spent a couple of weeks whining about how lonely I was, and finally Jim Ross fixed me up with a friend of his, Bill Fralic, who was like the starting tackle for the Atlanta Falcons. He was real sweet, even a little shy. Actually, I've been with a few football players, and they tend to be like that. Maybe because if you're a football player, you trot out onto the field wearing a helmet and pads, and then you're in a huddle with ten other guys, so

With Jim Plunkett, Super Bowl hero

you're kind of hidden. Whereas if you're a wrestler, it's just you — I mean, you're *out there*, practically naked, and you've got to put yourself over to a crowd of people staring straight at you. You develop like a hard edge, a callous; it affects the way you deal with the people in your life.

So Bill was a definite change of pace when we began to date. He was even bigger than John Tatum — the guy was six foot six, three hundred pounds. He took care of my man gap. When he got out of bed to pee in the middle of the night, you knew it; you'd hear him stomping down the hall towards the bathroom; I mean, the lamp on the night table shook.

Plus, he peed like Secretariat.

About a month after Bill and I started to date, I signed divorce papers from Eddie; I was kind of shocked when he told me he'd started the paperwork so soon, but both of us realized the marriage was over. I guess he was just being realistic. Still, it was kind of a slap in the face, and I was depressed for days afterwards. But then, one morning, for reasons known only to him, Eddie decided to show up at my apartment. Maybe he'd heard that I had a new boyfriend, and he was jealous. Or maybe he thought it was a wrestler, and he was just curious to find out who it was. Whatever the reason, he drove over one morning and didn't stop at the security gate. He parked his car down the road, then hopped the gate, and then he came around to my apartment. He must have seen Bill's car parked in the guest spot next to mine.

Well, I'm cooking breakfast in the kitchen when I hear a rattling noise in front of the door. So I rush to the door and open it. All I find is Buff Bagwell's barbecue grill turned over on its side. The tongs and spatula are thrown in different directions, and I'm staring down at the thing, wondering what the hell is going on. Then, a few seconds later, Buff opens his door, and now we're both staring down at the grill, like, *Huh?*

Then suddenly Sasha Girl darts out the door, all barking and happy, and she goes running around the corner. Then next thing I know, Eddie comes running back towards the door, yelling "All right, where is he? Where is the son-of-a-bitch?"

He pushes past me and runs into the apartment.

That's when Bill walks out of the bedroom. He's just gotten up, still yawning. He's wearing his underwear. And now he's staring down at Eddie, who's staring back up at him. Remember, Bill's half a foot taller than Eddie, and like seventy-five pounds heavier.

Bill says, "You got a problem with me?"

Now, suddenly, Eddie's like, "No, no problem. Hi, nice to meet you. You're that football guy, right? I'm a big fan of yours."

Bill starts to smile. "I could tell."

Then Eddie says, "Look, I'm really sorry we have to meet like this."

But Bill's really easygoing, you know, good-natured, so he says, "Hey, man, it's tough. I've been there."

Now Eddie glances back over his shoulder. "I kind of made a mess with your grill."

"It's not my grill."

Then Buff calls in from outside. "It's my grill!"

Which cracks all of us up.

Eddie calls back, "Sorry, guy."

The end of the story is that Bill and Eddie kind of bonded. He wound up walking Eddie out to his car. When he didn't come back for ten minutes, I went outside and peeked around the corner of the gate. There were the two of them, talking away; finally, they shook hands. That was when I rushed back inside. I figured it was a guy moment. Not the kind of thing I was supposed to see.

Except now I'm writing about it.

God, I *am* a bitch!

I stopped seeing Bill a month or so later. It had nothing to do with what happened that morning. It was more like we just didn't work together — as a couple, I mean. Hey, the guy owned an insurance company. I didn't see myself with a guy who owned an insurance company. It would be like if Cher was sleeping with Dan Rather. You'd think about the two of them together, and you'd think: *What's wrong with this picture?*

But Bill kind of got me started on a football player kick. The names are long gone, but I think I went out on dates with a couple of Falcons, and then, I think, a Cincinnati Bengal. Maybe there was a Chicago Bear mixed in. But I do remember, I developed a major crush on Jim Kelly, the Buffalo Bills quarterback. I saw him on television after the Bills lost the Super Bowl in 1991, and he just had this heartbroken, hang-dog look about him, and it got to me. So I sent him a Missy promo picture along with a note that said, "I want to meet you."

He called me up about a week later and told me he followed wrestling, he knew who I was, and he wanted to meet me too. We talked on the phone for hours that first night; I mean, we just clicked. He was going to be in Atlanta to shoot a commercial for an eyeglass company the next month, so we arranged to have lunch.

Naturally, I was real excited about it at first. The guy just quarterbacked the *Super Bowl*. But the more I thought about it, the more hopeless the situation seemed. No way was I shuttling back and forth to Buffalo. And I knew for sure he wasn't about to relocate to Atlanta.

So I figured I'd just have a quiet lunch with him, maybe rent a room afterwards, but I realized, long term, nothing was going to happen between me and Jim Kelly. I called him back the next day, and we spoke for a long time.

We wound up having lunch with my friend Elix, talking about the Grateful Dead. I mean, it was so platonic I could have puked. But we stayed in touch. I sent him a Missy Hyatt T-shirt, and he wore it a couple of times for national interviews. I got a big kick out of that.

It was the next Sunday after the phone call from Jim Kelly that I came home from a skiing trip in Tennessee and found two messages on my answering machine. I'd been gone since Friday night, and I just wanted to take a nap, but I figured I'd better listen to the messages. The first was twenty-four hours old, from Saturday afternoon, from a guy named Wade. He said he was a publicist who worked at WCW; he said Jason Hervey was in town and wanted to know if I would have dinner with him.

As I was listening to the message, I was thinking, *Jason who?*

Then second message was only a couple of hours old, from Sunday morning. I think the exact words were: "Hello, this is Jason Hervey. I'm leaving town tonight. My flight's at ten o'clock. I was just wondering if maybe the two of us could grab a bite to eat before that. Whatever...."

Then he left his phone number at the hotel.

Now I was curious. The "whatever" got to me. It sounded confident, you know? So I called up my girlfriend Elix and asked her if she'd ever heard of Jason Hervey. She started yelling, "Oh my God! That's the kid on *The Wonder Years*!"

"The TV show?"

"Yeah!"

"But that kid must be like thirteen."

"No, not him. You're thinking of Fred Savage. The kid who plays the older brother. I don't know his name in the show. 'Butthead' or something. But that's not it. That's just what Fred Savage calls him. He's kind of a hottie."

I hung up with Elix and phoned Jason Hervey's hotel room. He sounded very young over the phone, like a kid, and I almost backed out, but we talked for maybe fifteen minutes — and once I got past the voice, I started to realize I liked him.

Finally, we arranged to meet at the Buckhead Diner — a half mile from my apartment.

I got there first and took a booth in the back. I recognized him as soon as he walked in. Actually, he looked older than he sounded, older than I remembered him from *The Wonder Years*. He was short, five foot seven, husky but not fat. He had a handsome face. He spotted me and waved, then walked over to the booth. I guess what impressed me, what surprised me to be honest, was how down-to-earth he was. The way he spoke to the waiter, looked him in the eye, like he was talking to his buddy. Then two girls came over to us during dinner; they were sisters, probably like twelve and fourteen year old. Real giggly. They had no idea who I was, which kind of bugged me. But I remember Jason talked to them for like five minutes. Signed autographs for them. I mean, I knew he wanted to be alone with me. Plus, I knew he only had a couple of hours before his flight. But he took the time to make them feel special. I know, if it had been me, and I only had a couple of hours to score with a guy, I'd have been shooing them away. But he kept smiling and chatting away with the girls until their parents called them back to their table.

So we had dinner, and then we talked, and then I invited him back to my place. I guess it goes without saying that he wound up missing his flight.

Actually, he didn't leave my apartment for four days.

Jason and I dated for about two years. Hands down, the best boyfriend I ever had — which, as you've probably figured out, is saying a mouthful. But the weird thing was, no one outside our circle of friends actually believed we were a real couple. We made a few tabloid papers, and then a few gossip columns, but when the wrestling magazines picked up on the story, fans wrote in that the relationship was just an angle. I mean, he was eighteen and I was twenty-six. Plus, I was three inches taller than he was — and when I wore heels, I towered over him. I think he was more self-conscious about the height thing than the age thing. I used to say to him, "Hey, if you stand on your wallet, you're taller than anyone in the room." But he knew the wrestlers used to rib me about him. Like they'd say, "Hey, Missy, where's your little guy?" Or else they would start whistling that munchkin song from *The Wizard of Oz*. And God help me if I went out to dinner with the Steiners and ordered shrimp!

What pissed me off, though, was the jokes were always behind his back. No one ever said a thing to his face. No, whenever Jason was around, the wrestlers would kiss up to him. They'd drape their arms over his shoulders and say, "Hey, maybe you can get me a shot on *The Wonder Years*." Plus, his mother was a big time Hollywood agent. So just about every week one of them would hand him a head shot and ask him to show the photo to his mom. Eric Bischoff was the worst. Whenever Jason was in town, Bischoff was all over him like ugly on a gorilla. That's Bischoff's thing; he's always dreamed about a career in Hollywood. I don't even know what he'd do there. Maybe produce movies — I guess that's his wet dream. Because he loves the glitz. So he's always kissing up to people with connections. Which is why, years later, he was hanging around with Hulk Hogan. It wasn't the wrestling. It was because Hogan had friends in Hollywood.

Anyway, like I said, Jason was the best boyfriend I ever had. Treated me like a queen. I loved his family. His mom and his dad. They never had a problem with the fact that I was older than he was. I remember his mom took me aside the first time we met and asked how old I was. I knew Jason had told her that I was twenty-four. But I said, "Look, I can't lie to you. I'm twenty-six." She just cracked up and told me that Jason always went for

TED AND MISSY'S BOGUS JOURNEY

Jason Hervey, his hog, and, oh yes, me

older women. Both his parents were just so sweet to me. I even met his grandmother and grandfather. I picked up the expression *Oy vey!* from hanging around with his grandfather.

Looking back, maybe the reason the age difference *didn't* matter was because we were both still just kids. We always used to pull pranks. Real juvenile stuff, I mean. Like we'd drive up to the Playboy Mansion and yell into the intercom: "Condom delivery for Miss July!" Then speed off. (Yeah, yeah, I know how lame it sounds!) Another time we drove past Aaron Spelling's house, and Jason jumped out of the car and peed on his lawn.

He also taught me how to ride a Harley. I'd ridden motorcycles before, but they were just kind of souped up scooters. Jason bought me a Harley Sportster and taught me how to ride it one afternoon in the parking lot of the Hollywood Bowl. That night, I was white-lining it — you know, riding between cars — down Sunset Boulevard.

After six months, I actually picked up and moved to Los Angeles. Jason bought a house in West Hollywood, close to Century City. It was a beautiful house, real sunny, lots of light. And I negotiated with WCW so that I would only have to be in Atlanta one day a week; I wasn't managing at that point, just announcing and interviewing, so I'd tape my segments, back to back, for like eight hours, and then I'd fly back to L.A. that night.

It was real expensive, flying back and forth, but when I was with Jason, for the first time in my life, I didn't have to think about money. I know that's not a very romantic thing to say. I know I should say how crazy in love we were, how we would have been happy together even if we were both broke. But looking back, to be truthful, I'd have to say money was a big part of our relationship. Between my salary with WCW and promotional appearances I was making decent money myself, but it was nothing compared to what Jason was raking in. I mean, he was making serious money. The guy made more per episode on *The Wonder Years* than I made in like six months. Plus, he was being merchandised non-stop. Lunch boxes. Note book covers. That kind of stuff. It was like every morning I'd walk out to the mailbox, and there would be three checks. They just kept rolling in.

Even so, Jason was constantly complaining about how hard he had to work. It used to get on my nerves. I mean, basically, he was getting paid to say a couple of lines, burp and get called "Butthead." I remember one time he came home and was whining about how he had to eat eight

Party at the Playboy Mansion: Top, wth Pia and Elix, above with Sandra Bernhardt and left, with Elix and Tony Curtis

spoonfuls of peanut butter because Fred Savage or somebody kept screwing up lines. I looked Jason in the eye and said, "You know, for as much money as you're getting paid, I'd let them stick peanut butter up my butt!"

Still, I didn't save a nickel the entire two years we were together. I'm sure Jason's accountant was looking out for him, squirreling away a percentage of his paycheck each week from *The Wonder Years* — which is lucky, because whatever money we saw, we spent. You could almost hear the *wooosh* as it came and went. I mean, we'd drive out to the malls together and do *serious* damage. We flew into New York City one afternoon and spent eight thousand dollars in an hour at Barney's. Then we rushed back to the hotel room, laid out all the loot across the bed and made love. That was probably the best sex I've ever had. Rolling around on Ferragamo shoes and Chanel purses. I was screaming so loud that people were giggling in the hotel hallway.

That was the weekend I fell in love with New York. I was in town for a couple of autograph sessions, and Jason was on hiatus, so we spent three days in Manhattan. Shopping on West 57th Street. Rollerblading in Central Park. Riding past Rockefeller Center at twilight in a horse-drawn carriage. It was like something you'd read about in a novel.

🍸

It was Jason who got me interested in hockey. He was a big time L.A. Kings fan. Bought season tickets every year. Bought one for me too, but for the longest time I hated going. The games bored me to tears; I used to sit rinkside and read a book. The scratching sounds of the skates against the ice used to drive me up the wall. Plus, the fans were so bloodthirsty — literally, I mean; the entire crowd used to jump to their feet whenever a fight broke and scream "Kill the motherfucker!" or just "Go! Go! Go!" They made wrestling fans look like freaking Buddhists. Plus, I couldn't stand being around hockey players — I used to call them gerbils because their hair was always long in the back, like a gerbil's tail, and it stayed matted down for hours after the game. Hockey hair. So we'd go out to dinner after the game with like Luc Robitaille, and he'd be ordering his meal, and I'd be thinking, *What a freaking gerbil!*

Eventually, though, I came around. Or at least I got to a point where I didn't bring a book to the games. I'd shmooze a lot. There was kind of a celebrity row at Kings games. Me and Jason. Alan Thicke. Richard Dean Anderson — the guy who played MacGyver. Kelsey Grammer used to show up occasionally.

I remember once Jason and I and Alan Thicke and Richard Dean Anderson were jammed together in the back of a limo after a celebrity game, and Anderson was jumping up and down, messing with the radio, trying to figure out how turn it on without the remote control. But he couldn't do it. He kept giving up, falling back into the seat next to Jason, and then, a minute later, he'd decide to try again. Finally, after about the fifth time, Jason yelled at him, "Dammit, Anderson, you're *MacGyver*! You can make an airplane out of a stick of gum, but you can't figure out how to turn on a damn car radio!"

Unfortunately, as I was changing my opinion about hockey, I was also changing my opinion about hockey players. I started to like them.

And when I say *unfortunately*, I mean, *unfortunately for me and Jason*.

It was around the time we celebrated the second anniversary of our dinner at the Buckhead Diner in Atlanta. We'd been drifting apart for months. I didn't like living in Los Angeles. I missed my friends in Atlanta, I missed the change of seasons, and I hated flying back and forth every week. I mean, it wasn't just the hours in the air. I'd be jet-lagged for two days afterwards. It was affecting my stomach. I couldn't eat at normal times. And I wasn't sleeping.

Basically, I was miserable, and I began taking it out on Jason. I'd start in on him the second he walked through the door — about nothing. He would come home, and I'd just pick a fight. He was so good-natured that sometimes I had a hard time getting him going. Like, once I began yelling at him because he slammed the door. He didn't, really. He just shut it slightly harder than usual. But I tore into him. And he cracked up. Right in my face, he cracked up. Which pissed me off even more, and I got right up in his face. But I couldn't get a rise out of him. Finally, I stormed out of the house and spent the night in a hotel.

It was around our second anniversary, like I said, that I cheated on him. With a hockey player. I was in to Philadelphia to visit my friend Cathy, who was also a big hockey fan, and she had tickets for a Flyers

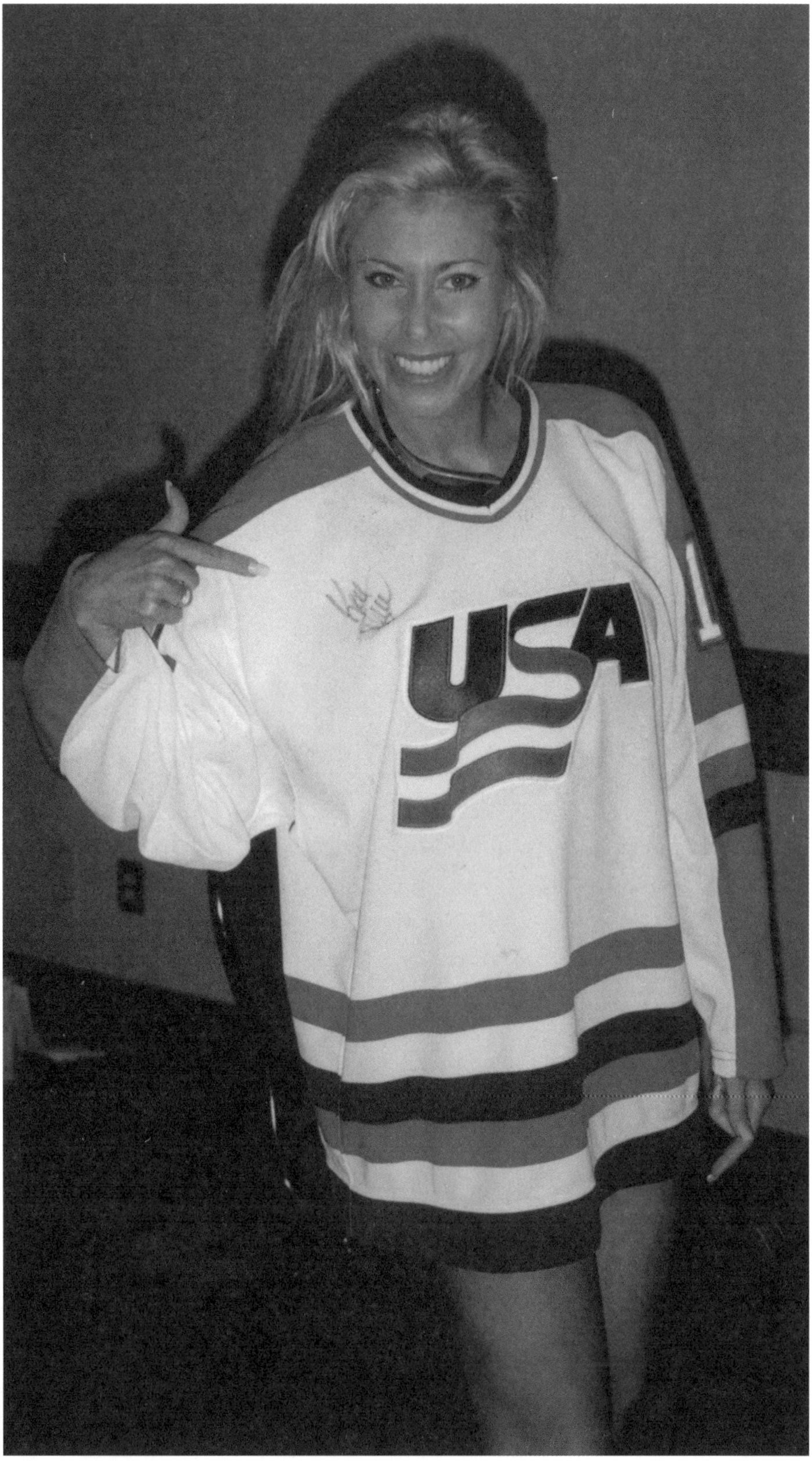
USA

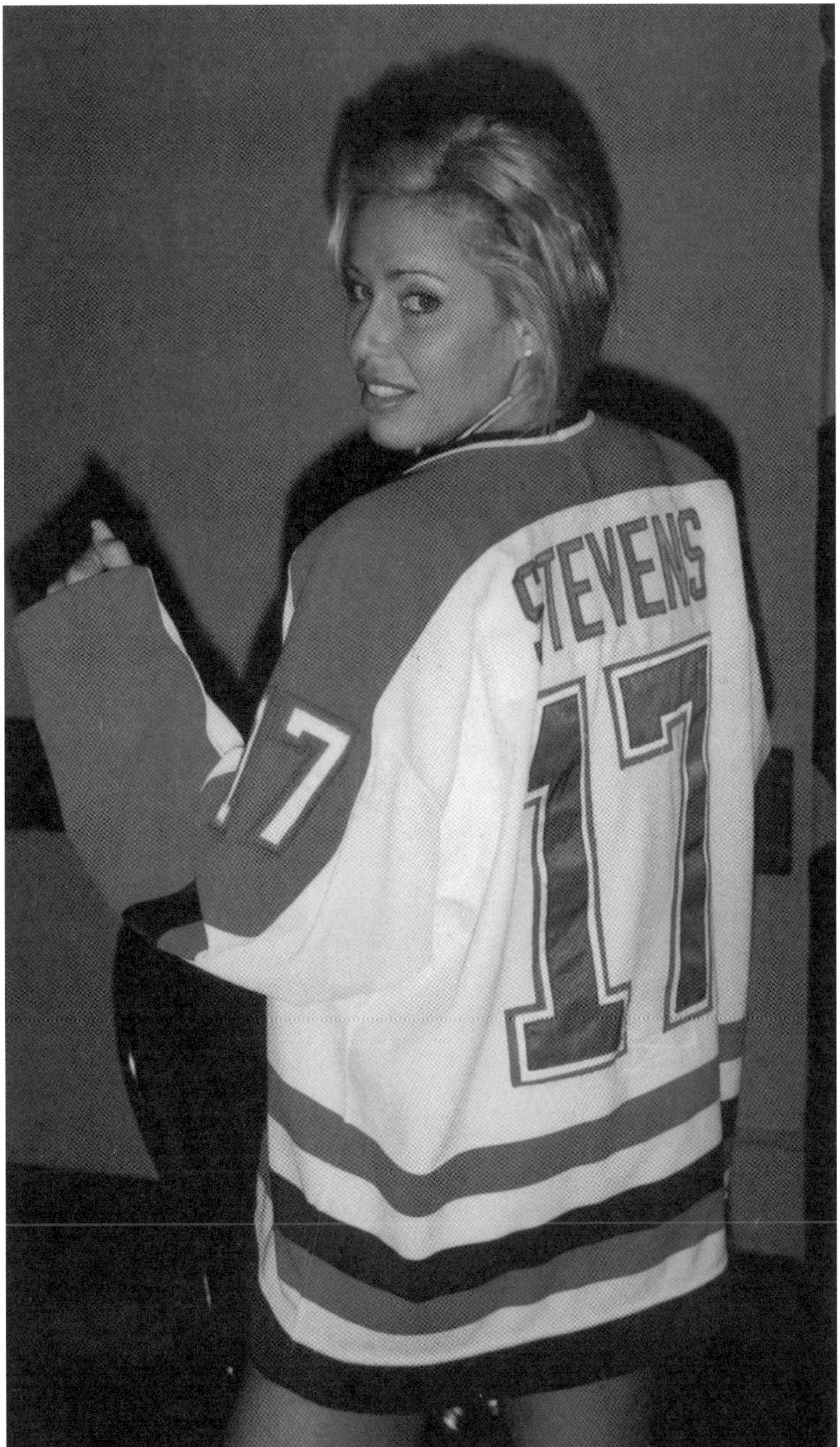
STEVENS
17

game; going to another hockey game was just about the *last* thing I wanted to do, but she dragged me there, and afterwards she introduced me to Rod Brind'Amour. Well, it turned out he was a wrestling fan, and the three of us went out to dinner, and then Cathy left the two of us alone, and . . . well, you can guess what happened. I mean, they guy was ripped; he had the most awesome set of abs I'd ever seen. Even his butt was ripped; it had deep indentations on the sides, where the cheeks hit the thigh muscles. The only bad thing was you kind of had to put a bag over his head — mentally, I mean — because his face was all messed up. His nose had been broken like eight times, and he had scars on his forehead and chin and underneath his jaw. He kind of looked like Frankenstein. Except with Brad Pitt's body. And gerbil hair.

When I got back to L.A., I felt real guilty about what happened. But I kept quiet for a week. Then, when I couldn't take it anymore, I confessed to Jason. That's what finally broke us up. Psychologically, I guess, I did it on purpose. Had the affair, I mean. I didn't want to live in California, I didn't want to keep flying back and forth, so I screwed Rod Brind'Amour.

Yeah, I could have handled it better.

The thing was, after two years with Jason, I'd kind of forgotten that he was still just twenty-one. The break up reminded me. Before I told him about Rod Brind'Amour, I'd convinced myself that he would take it well, that he would immediately grasp the fact that the we had drifted apart, that the writing was already on the wall for us as a couple. I was wrong. I guess, when you're twenty-one, that's just not how you think. You think you'll never fall out of love — or you think, if you do fall out of love, you'll fall out of love together. It won't just be one of you. So it was real teary when I told him. Real moany. He got hurt the way a kid gets hurt.

Less than a week later, I moved back to Atlanta. Jason arranged to ship all my stuff, even the stuff he had bought me. The BMW. The Harley. Boxes and boxes of clothes. He made the arrangements himself. That made me feel worse, how brave he was being.

Then I started opening the boxes of clothes.

He peed on my clothes — every single box.

I mean, I don't get that.

What is it with guys and peeing? First, it was that stupid dog, Buddy. Then the Freebirds.
Then Jason Hervey.

Throughout the time I was with Jason, Jim Kelly would call me every so often. He knew nothing was going to happen, but we used to flirt over the phone. And he would leave messages just to make Jason jealous, like, "Hey, Missy, it's Jim. You left your panties under the seat of my car. Do you want me to FedEx them or what?" He did it like half a dozen times. Even Jason had to laugh at some of them.

But after Jason and I broke up, I began calling Jim more often. The fact that we'd been flirting over the phone for two years — I mean, there was no way we *weren't* going to get together. It was just a matter of our schedules.

Well, it was like God worked out the timing us. The Super Bowl was set for Atlanta in 1994, and the Bills were in the playoffs, so all Jim had to do was keep winning to wind up in Atlanta for an entire week. It was like a carnival game, and I was the grand prize. Or booby prize, whatever. (All right, yeah, I guess he wanted that championship ring too!) Every week, he'd call me right after his playoff game, and he'd be like, "Two down, one to go."

Well, he wound up making the Super Bowl. (You Bills fans can send me thank you notes if you want!) It was like the fourth straight year the Bills made it — except the thing was, they lost the first three times. So by the time he arrived in Atlanta, he was under unbelievable pressure. We arranged to have dinner three nights before the game, but I could tell as soon as he showed up that he wasn't himself. It was like the lights were on inside his head, but no one was home. He tried to smile and say flirty things, but every ten minutes, his mind would wander, and he would be somewhere else. I felt bad for him.

Half way through dinner, a reporter from a Pittsburgh newspaper walked into the restaurant, and he noticed us together. He started scribbling notes — because Pittsburgh was Jim's home town, so his social life was big news. The story ran in the gossip column the next morning.

After dinner, I drove us back to his hotel, and then we ran upstairs to his room, sat down on the bed and started kissing. Then, maybe a minute later, I feel him kind of shudder against me. Then he whispers, "Oh, excuse me." I looked down, and he'd come in his pants. I mean, all we did was kiss! Never even got to second base. I thought it was sweet, but he was so annoyed at himself. After two years of anticipation, the big moment finally arrives — and then it's over in less than a minute. He limps out.

I mean, no wonder he never won a Super Bowl!

(He'll probably kill me for telling that story.)

Sorry, Jim.

Maybe the worst thing about the break up with Jason was that it pissed off Eric Bischoff, who by then was running WCW. Like I said, he used to kiss up to Jason every chance he got — he even used Jason's connections to pitch some lame-ass kids' show he'd dreamed up — but now he couldn't plant his lips on Jason's butt anymore. So he took it out on me. I was floating around in the organization, announcing a little, managing a little, but I had no definite role. Well, Bischoff decided that I would be a full time manager. Which was fine with me. When he called me into his office and told me he wanted me to manage, I suggested that he put me with the Hollywood Blondes, Brian Pillman and Stunning Steve Austin. (Yes, *that* Steve Austin; this was 1994, long before he went "Stone Cold.") I mean, it made perfect sense. I was blond. I was just back from Hollywood. Who better to manage the Hollywood Blondes?

Instead, Bischoff put me with the Nasty Boys, Brian Knobbs and Jerry Saggs. They were nice guys, mid-card guys, decent workers. I had nothing against them, but their gimmick made no sense whatsoever with my character. They were supposed to be out-of-control hardcore punks. And I was supposed to be, well, *Missy*. But I didn't have the energy to argue. So I wound up cutting my hair real short, wearing black fishnet dresses with glow-in-the-dark pink bras underneath, and I'd be cracking a bull whip as I walked down the aisle on the way to the ring. I mean, Missy, with a bull whip? It was just so butch!

Whatever happened to the Gucci purse?

So Bischoff stuck me with the Nasty Boys, and I figured we'd be wrestling mid-card indefinitely. Every week, I trotted out to the ring with

The Nasty Boys with me on the ropes

the Nasties like a good little soldier, gut sucked in, boobs up high, distracted their opponents, and then headed home. Didn't complain once. What I didn't count on was the Nasties getting the World Tag title. You see, Dusty's wife's sister was married to Jerry Saggs . . . so you figure it out. That's how the business works. You get a push because you're family. Or because you kiss ass. Or because you give the booker head.

So the Nasties wound up becoming tag team champions.

Just like *that*, I'm back working main events. But Bischoff was still out to screw me over. He gave me no TV time whatsoever. No interviews. No bits between matches. He even told the announcers not to mention that I was ringside with the Nasty Boys. The camera guys weren't supposed to shoot me. It was like I wasn't even there.

All I was doing was dressing up like a sleazy punk, walking out to the ring, and picking up a paycheck at the end of the week.

Meanwhile, my personal life was a mess. After the break up with Jason, I kind of spun out of control. Guys who I'd have never given a second look, I woke up next to. I spent a couple of nights with Scott Levy — yeah, Raven. The joke of it was, this was years after we did the angle in Memphis where I promised him a date if he could beat Jerry Lawler.

And he never did beat Lawler, but he got laid.

After Raven, it was Eric Watts — Bill Watts's son, remember? But like I said, I slept with him mainly because I knew it would piss off his father, and because I didn't have time to do my laundry that week.

After Eric Watts, it was Road Warrior Hawk. It was the second go round with Hawk; I'd slept with him years before, right after Jake Roberts dumped me, since he was Jake's best friend. Hawk and I stayed in touch through the years, almost by accident, because our paths kept crossing. Actually, he was one of only two wrestlers who ever complimented me on my work. (The other, incidentally, was Marc Mero — Sable's husband . . . and, *no*, I didn't sleep with him! You hear that, Sable? You glommed my gimmick, but I didn't glom your man.) I dated Hawk for a couple of months; I even used my night on the WCW 900-Hotline to talk about him — you know, like free p.r. His tag line was always "Snack on danger! Dine on death!" So I'd go on the 900 line and say "Last Friday night, Road Warrior Hawk snacked on danger, dined on death . . . and then he had Missy for dessert."

Except then he dumped me!

Now that *really* pissed me off. It felt like Jake was dumping me all over again. So I did what any woman would do. Or at least any woman with her own 900 number. I started ragging on him, making fun of the shape of his skull. I called him the Road Wart Hog. The next week, there were a dozen Wart Hog posters scattered throughout the crowd.

After Hawk, it was hockey players, hockey players, hockey players. Then back to wrestling with Ed Leslie — who wrestled as Brutus Beefcake. I met him through mutual friends of ours, the Bushwackers. . . .

(Guess what? I just had a kind of out-of-body experience. I heard the words I just wrote inside my head, and I flashed back to when I was a little girl. What are the chances that little Melissa Hiatt would ever grow up and talk about how she met a guy named "Brutus Beefkcake" through her friends "the Bushwackers"?)

So, anyway, the Bushwackers invited me to their beach house in Clearwater, Florida, and Brutus was there. He was telling stories about riding his Harley and working with the WWF, so the two of us hit it off. He was up front about the fact that he was involved with another woman. (Actually, I think he wound up marrying her.) But we had a good time together for like maybe a month. What I remember most about Brutus was one afternoon when we were driving down to Sarasota, Florida, with Hulk Hogan — who was Brutus's best friend. The three of us were on our way to pick up Hogan's Harley Davidson, and out of nowhere Hulk turns to me and says, "Yo, Missy, I'm going to start my own wrestling company. You going to come work for me?"

And I'm like, "You going to pay me more than I'm making?"

He smiles at me and shoots back, "Hey, I always pay people what they're worth."

So I start laughing and say, "No deal."

"Why not?"

"Because if we ever got paid what we were really worth, we'd all be just a bunch of broken down jaybronees."

🍸

I guess I could have continued to manage the Nasty Boys indefinitely. The fact that Bischoff tried to keep me off camera didn't bother me very much. The fans knew who I was; hey, you couldn't pick up a wrestling magazine

Auditioning for Executive-of-the-Year!

without me somewhere in it. I was kind of jaded; it wasn't as much fun as it used to be back when I was starting out in the business. But between my salary, merchandizing and promotional fees, I was making six figures.

Then it happened.

I was working a pay-per-view with the Nasty Boys. They were wrestling Sting and Road Warrior Hawk. (How's that for ironic!) The match was for the tag team title.

Things were weird from the start. During the introductions, I was taunting the opponents, you know, gesturing at them, pointing to the belts around the Nasty Boys' waists, like, *Take a good look, fellas! You'll never wear these! They're ours!* It was part of our standard pre-match routine. But then, suddenly, I look up, and I notice Hawk is grinning. I mean, that's exactly what he was supposed to be doing — grinning at me, not taking me seriously. Except, at that moment, it seemed like he was really grinning at me. Because he'd just dumped me a month before. So during the match, I kept begging the Nasties to toss him out of the ring near me . . . so I could slap him. That's what happened too. I slapped him so hard, the fans in the first three rows all jumped out of their seats. And they're like, *Whoa!*

They knew it was real because they heard it.

Now Hawk's rubbing his cheek, and he's got this amazed expression, you know, his eyes bugging out, but then a second later he starts to smile again, and he says to me, under his breath, "That was a shoot, man!"

That snapped me out of it. I got this sheepish look on my face and just kind of slinked back to my corner.

So the match itself keeps going, and for a time, things are running as planned. Tag in, tag out. Heat on us, heat on them. Real uneventful. But then, about fifteen minutes in, Saggs tags in Knobbs . . . and then Saggs rolls out of the ring under the bottom rope. That gets my attention because he's supposed to climb through the ropes and stand on the ring apron, waiting to get tagged back in. I rush over to him, and he's clutching his knee. He's hurt. For real, I mean. The knee's already starting to swell up like a cantaloupe.

He looks up at me and says, "I'm done. I'm done. You gotta get in there!"

What he means is that the match is booked to end in a disqualification. That way, the Nasties keep the belts, but Sting and Hawk stay the number one contenders. Except at that moment, Sting is body-slamming

With Hawk

Knobbs and covering him for a pin. Saggs is supposed to jump in and break up the count. Sting's expecting it. Knobbs is expecting it. The ref's expecting it. He's diving down next to Sting and Knobbs and starting his three count . . . and of course once he starts the three count, he can't stop just because the match is booked to end one way. Once he gets to two, and his hand starts coming down for the third count, he's committed.

It's like the entire scene is happening in slow motion. The crowd's jumping to their feet, the ref's starting the count, I can see him forming the word "one" with his mouth, and Sting's hooking Knobb's leg for the pin, and all three of them are kind of glancing out of the corners of their eyes, waiting for Saggs to come through the ropes and break up the count.

Except Saggs can't even stand up.

He yelling at me, "Get in there! You gotta get in there!"

Without thinking, I jump onto the ring apron and dive in between the ropes, and a second later, I'm on Sting's back, yanking his hair, breaking up the ref's three count at about two and three quarters.

Sting leaps up, and now I'm riding him piggyback around the ring.

With Brutus Beefcake

Meanwhile, the ref has figured out that Saggs must be hurt, so he's waving his arms, calling for the bell.

We've got the disqualification.

I hear the bell, and I start letting go of Sting's hair.

That's when he flips me over his shoulder, up in the air and then boom down onto the mat. Right on my butt. It's no big deal. I sell it, you know, roll around and groan for a couple of seconds, then stand up and start rubbing my butt, but I'm fine.

Suddenly, the first few rows of fans are roaring.

I mean, it's not just the average pop from the crowd at the end of a title match; it's like only the first three rows. Flashbulbs are lighting up ringside, and I'm looking behind me and off to both sides, trying to figure out what's going on.

Finally, I hear Hawk's voice behind me, "Missy!"

I turn around.

"Kayfabe your breast! Kayfabe your breast!"

Then I look down.

My left boob has popped out.

The nipple is showing over the top of the pink bra, like it's peering out at the crowd through the mesh dress. My first reaction is like, *Whoop-dee-damn-doo.* So my boob's hanging out. It's happened before while I was rolling around, catfighting. It's not something I'm going to lose sleep about.

Except then I remember this is a live pay-per-view.

I cover up real quick with my arms and spin away from the camera as I'm tucking the boob back inside the bra. I stamp my feet, and then I rush over to Knobbs and start punching him in the shoulders and chest, like it's his fault I was humiliated.

Meanwhile, I'm thinking: *Just another day at the office.*

It was about a month later that the Nasty Boys and I showed up at the CNN Center to pose for a new set of promo pictures. We're headed upstairs and then through a long hallway that led to the photography studio. Outside the door of the studio, there's a bulletin board covered with Polaroids of network personalities. There's a photo of Larry King, and there's Wolf Blitzer, and there's Bernard Shaw, and there's . . .

Me with my left boob hanging out!

I mean, there it is, in living color, enlarged to eight inches by eleven, and tacked up on the bulletin board between Polaroids of Bernard Shaw and Flip Spiceland.

Well, I just lost it!

I snatched the photograph off the bulletin board and flung it into a trash can at the end of the hall. But then, a second later, I reached back into the trash and took it out.

I had a hunch I might need it.

The next morning, I stormed into Eric Bischoff's office with the photo to complain, and he just nodded his head, like he could care less. He said he would try to find out who took it; I mean, I wanted the negative and all the copies.

For a week, I waited.

And waited. . . .

And waited. . . .

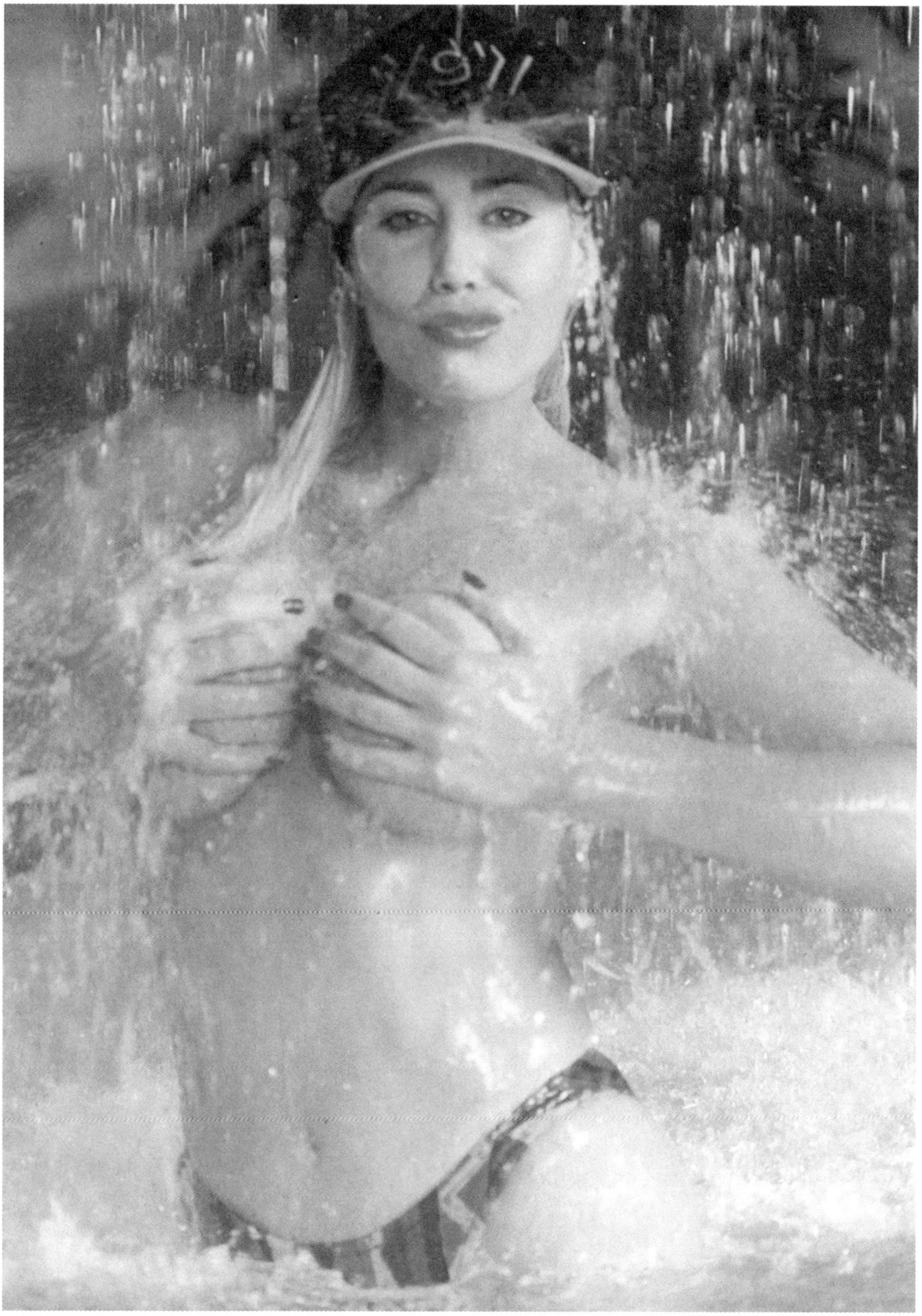

The thought that guys in suits, you know, corporate executives, were walking past a photograph of my breast and snickering — I mean, it was just gnawing at me. I called Bischoff a couple of times to ask what was happening, whether he'd found out who did it, and he said he was still looking into the matter. Then, after a week, I got fed up. I was in Orlando at a TV taping and called and complained to Bischoff's boss — a vice president with the Turner organization.

The next day, after the taping in Orlando, Bischoff fired me.

Bischoff fired me, basically, because I went over his head. I talked to his boss. He made an example out of me. He wanted to send a message to the rest of the on-air personalities and wrestlers, like: *I don't care who you are or how long you've been here; if you ever go over my head, I'll fire you.* Plus, of course, he was still trying to keep up his friendship — if you want to call it that — with Jason Hervey.

Well, I did what any good citizen would do under the circumstances.

I turned around and sued his ass.

That's like the American way, right?

Honestly, though, I just wanted my merchandising money. They owed me all kinds of money, and I sued to get it. Just to give you an idea, one year I earned fourteen thousand dollars from 20 percent of the profits on my 900 hotline; the next year, the numbers for the hotline were up, but I got a check for fifty dollars — for the entire year. No explanation. Plus, I sold all ten thousand copies of my 1994 calendar; I was supposed to get a third of the price for every calendar, and I never saw a cent. Not one red cent.

So I sued for the merchandising money. Except then, when I told my lawyer about the picture of my boob at CNN Center, she threw in sexual harassment.

Which is when the shit hit the fan.

There's not much I'm allowed to mention about the outcome of the lawsuit I filed against World Championship Wrestling. Legally, I mean. So I've got

"Let me at 'em!"

to pick my words carefully. All right, here goes: *The litigation was concluded, after approximately 18 months, in December 1996, and I am very pleased with the outcome.*

Sorry, guys, that's all I can tell you. Court orders. I don't mean to be a tease about it, but what can I say?

I signed a sheet of paper.

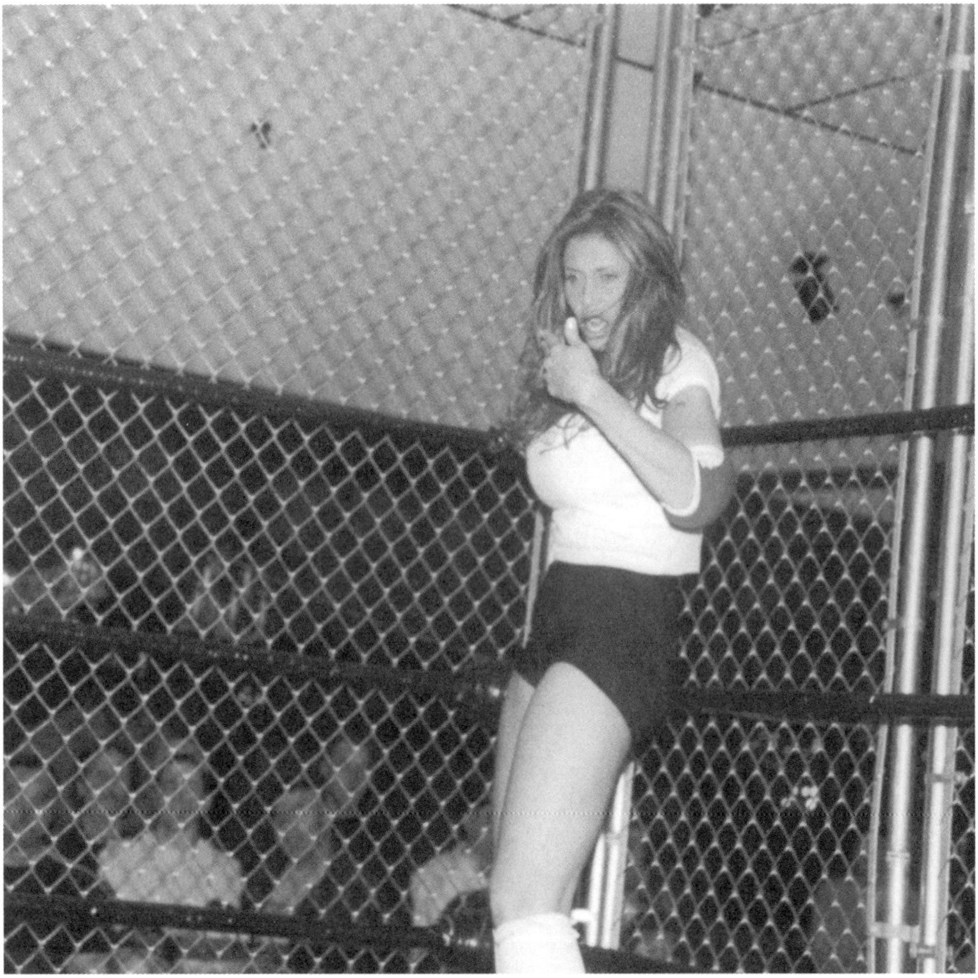

8

Taken to the Extreme

New York and Pennsylvania, ECW

So, anyway, Eric Bischoff fired me after a television taping in Orlando, and that night, at the Residence Inn, I called my mom and told her. She said good — it was the best thing that could've happened to me.

Then I called my best friend Elix, and the second I heard her voice, I burst out crying.

That's when the *real* depression kicked in. It all hit me, at once, I was *out of wresting*. I pissed off one guy, Eric Bischoff, and *woosh* I was gone. I heard that Bischoff was already making calls to replace me, and that tapped into all the insecurities I had about my place in wrestling history.

For a week in February 1994, I didn't leave my apartment in Atlanta. I didn't answer the phone. I didn't shower. I was eating soup crackers and drinking lukewarm tea, and I was swallowing handfuls of pills. Resteril. Ambian. Xanax. I didn't want to die. But I didn't want to get out of bed either.

Finally, Elix panicked and came over. She started yelling at me to get up, but I wouldn't budge. She called up Ed Leslie and told him to come over because she couldn't handle me alone. So then he showed up, and I told them both to leave me alone, but they dragged me out of bed, slapped me around and then shoved me into the shower. I don't know if she saved my life or not, but I'm pretty sure she saved my sanity.

No smart ass remarks, please!

That night, after I came out of it, I called Paul E. It was like three in the morning, and I was crying into the phone, telling him how I almost died, saying, "You know, when I die, I hope *The Wrestling Observer* is going to run like a two page write up on me. I hope they're going to talk about my impact on the business."

"No doubt about it."

"Because I did, you know. I *did* have an impact."

"Oh, definitely."

Then he started telling me about how he was working with Todd Gordon, who owned Eastern Championship Wrestling in Philadelphia. He said that he was going to turn it around, change the name to Extreme Championship Wrestling. He had big plans. It was going to be kickass hardcore wrestling, blood and guts. But I was real tired, so after like ten minutes I just set down the phone next to my head on the pillow, and I fell asleep listening to him going on and on about how he was going to turn the wrestling world on its ear.

I mean, it was just Paul E.

In April 1994, I moved to New York City. I didn't have a job lined up. I didn't have the slightest idea what I'd do. But I had good memories of Manhattan from when I was dating Jason Hervey, and I thought living there would cheer me up. The only contacts I had in the entire city were Paul E., who was still living up in Scarsdale, and a friend of Paul E.'s named Matt, who promoted parties at night clubs.

I found a little studio — and when I say a "little studio," I mean a teensy-weensy studio, like a walk-in closet with a refrigerator and a bathroom — on Columbus Avenue and 80th Street.

Let me tell you: I got to know the walls of that studio real well because for the first two weeks I was in New York, I sat in the apartment and stared at the walls. Actually, I alternated between the walls and the television. I watched a lot of soap operas. Hour after hour of them. The sun would be beaming in through the window, a perfect Spring afternoon, and I'd be glued to the TV, waiting for *All My Children* to start.

I spoke to Paul E. and Matt almost every day, and I tried to act cheerful, but I felt myself slipping back into the depression. Luckily, after that lost weekend in Atlanta, I'd flushed the rest of my pills down the toilet. So I was just sitting around, staring at the walls, watching soap operas. Paul E. would come over once a week and yell at me to get out of the house, and I would nod, like, *Tomorrow, I promise, I'll look for a job.*

But the next morning, I'd sleep until noon, then think to myself: *Well, it's too late to get going today. I'll start out fresh tomorrow.*

So, finally, Paul E. phoned Matt and said, "You've got to get her out of there." Then Matt made a couple of calls, and a week later I wound up working at Le Bar Bat — which is an upscale dance club and restaurant on West 57th Street.

It wasn't much of a job at first, just enough to get me out of the house a couple of times a week. I just made phone calls to promote Thursday night parties at the club. Actually, I could have done it from home, but the entire point — though of course I didn't realize it at the time — was to force me to put on clothes and come to work.

After a few weeks, Michael, the night manager, asked me if I wanted to tend bar. He told me the club needed a new bartender for the day shift, and he thought I'd be good at it. I said sure, so Rasi, the day manager, trained me behind the bar in the afternoon — when it wasn't hectic. Then she and Michael began working me during private parties so that I wouldn't have to ring up tabs. They broke me in slowly.

Finally, though, I started bartending nights at Le Bar Bat.

Yeah, I know, it doesn't sound like much, but tending bar was the first real trade I ever learned, the first professional skill I ever acquired that was useful outside a wrestling arena. I was earning enough money to survive, and I was earning it as Melissa, not Missy. I guess the word that comes to mind is *civilian*. I was earning money as a civilian.

It was Halloween of 1994 when a young guy came up to me at Le Bar Bat. I was coming off a fifteen minute break, and he tapped me on the shoulder just as I ducked back behind the bar. He was a stocky guy, in his early twenties, kind of cute but a little too young — even for me.

He said, "Excuse me, aren't you Missy Hyatt?"

"Yeah," I said, "I used to be. But now I'm your bartender. What can I get you to drink?"

"I know you."

"Lots of guys know me. I used to be Missy Hyatt. Now what can I get you to drink?"

"No, you don't understand. I'm Shane McMahon."

I stared at him for a second. "Vince's son?"

He nodded his head.

Well, I gave him a big hug, and later on that night we danced a couple of times downstairs, at the Halloween party, and he ended up giving me his phone number. Actually, I did call him. Not for a date though. Just to say hello, that kind of thing. He once got friends of mine tickets for a wrestling show at Madison Square Garden. He was just a real sweet guy.

The only reason I mention the fact that I met Shane McMahon at Le Bar Bat is because it kind of started me thinking that maybe I wanted to get back into wrestling — him being so nice, I mean. It made me realize that not everyone in the business was a scumbag. Not everyone was out to screw you, either literally or figuratively.

But the thing was, the lawsuit against WCW was still going on, the lawyers were still filing and counter-filing, and I knew no one was going to hire me until the litigation was over. I don't know if you'd say I was being blackballed. It was more like all the other promotions were kind of sitting back, waiting to see what happened. Naturally, no one wanted to piss off Ted Turner. That's the reason I never hit up Paul E. for a job with ECW. He might have done it, you know, as a favor for a friend, but then WCW might have come after him. Started signing his talent away.

That's how pro wrestling has always worked.

It was February 1995 when the worst phone call I ever got came on a Friday night. I was still bartending at Le Bar Bat, but I had off that night, and I remember I was about to call out for Chinese food. The phone rang while my hand was hovering over it. Even before I picked up the receiver, a chill ran through my body. I just had a bad feeling.

It was Paul E.

He said, "Missy, something's happened . . ."

He was talking real slow, real soft. I almost started to laugh when I heard the tone of his voice. I mean, it just sounded so odd to hear him not going a mile a minute.

Then he told me that Eddie was dead.

I started yelling at Paul E. while he was still saying the words. I didn't believe him. I told him it had to be a rumor, or else a bad joke, but he was crying into the phone, swearing on his life that it was true.

Finally, I slammed down the receiver.

Then I called Eddie's mother down in Tennessee, and she was crying when she picked up the phone. The second I heard her crying, I started to cry. I knew it was true.

Eddie Gilbert died of a heart attack in Puerto Rico. He had wrestled the night before. He went home, went to sleep, and he never woke up. He was 33 years old.

I don't remember much about the week after Eddie's death. Lots of people told me afterwards they called me to check in, but I don't remember talking to one of them. It's all a blur. I do remember calling my mom and asking her if she thought I should go to the funeral. I wanted to go, definitely. But Eddie's dad never liked me very much, and when our marriage ended, his dad blamed me for whatever bad happened to Eddie. He even blamed me for Eddie remarrying too soon after our divorce — he married a lady wrestler named Madusa less than a year later, and that marriage lasted about ten minutes. Their divorce was so nasty it made ours look like a picnic in the park.

So I called my mom and asked her whether I should go, and she told me to stay home. "You have to have respect for the living," she said. "If you know it will make the father uncomfortable, then you should stay away."

So I did: I stayed home.

I had a picture of our two dogs, Sasha Girl and Scooter, together, and I wrote a poem on the back of the photo and FedExed it to Eddie's mom

— and she put it in the casket. My parents and I sent flowers, and Bonnie Blackstone told me afterwards that our flowers were up front. She told me the church was packed, standing room only. People were lined up outside too.

It was Eddie's last show, and he sold out the house.

I paid my respects in my own way six months later. I went by and had lunch with his mom. I left flowers on Eddie's grave. It was a private moment. I mean, it wasn't a photo op. I knelt down, said a prayer, and then I got up and left.

You know, I told you at the beginning of this book that Melissa and Missy were mixed up together, that you couldn't understand one without understanding the other. But it wasn't Missy who was married to Eddie. It was Melissa. And it wasn't Missy who mourned him. It was Melissa. What I felt for Eddie and what he felt for me had nothing to do with what we did for a living. Two human beings fell in love, got married, fell out of love, got divorced . . . and then one of them died. There's no gimmick about that. There's no angle to work. "Hot Stuff Eddie Gilbert" didn't die. My ex-husband did.

And it hurt.

It wasn't until December, 1996, that my lawsuit against WCW was concluded, and I could start thinking seriously about getting back into wrestling. By then, Paul E.'s Extreme Championship Wrestling was up and running; it was the talk of the industry, pulling in ratings on weird little cable channels. It would be like the station manager would wake up and say, *Okay, Goober, get the hamster going, it's time for ECW.* I mean, at 12:59 a.m., there'd be twelve people watching a gay guy poach an egg, and then a minute later, the numbers for the station would jump to 10,000 viewers.

So in February 1997, Paul E. asked me to come back to work. I'd been nagging him for a couple of months. Then Nancy — you know, Kevin Sullivan's ex-wife, *Woman* — who was in ECW managing

Sandman, told Paul E. that she was going back to WCW. That meant a slot was opening up.

Which is when Paul E. called me.

Since I'd been out of the business for a couple of years, we needed to cook up an angle to bring me back. I mean, it wasn't like the fans didn't know what had been going on for the last two years. So Paul E. was sitting around, brainstorming, trying to figure out a storyline that would kind of acknowledge what had happened with the lawsuit, you know, like an inside joke, and also introduce me to the ECW audience.

Eventually, he came up with a real good angle.

Paul E. put me in a front row seat for an ECW taping in Queens, New York. I was with a girlfriend, and I was wearing sunglasses and a hat so none of the fans would recognize me in advance. Then, about half way through the show, a wrestler named Stevie Richards — who was like part wrestler, part ring clown — came walking down the aisle and stopped suddenly, right next to me.

Then he called for the ring microphone and said, "Whoa, wait just a minute. What have we here? Why, yes, I do believe we have a *major* celebrity in the audience. Ladies and gentlemen, please give a warm ECW welcome to . . . Missy Hyatt!"

So he tapped me on the shoulder and made me stand up and take a bow.

But then he started ragging on me, saying how much I wanted him. So I grabbed Richards by the hair, and then I planted a long wet kiss right on his mouth.

Now the fans start chanting, "She's hardcore! She's hardcore! She's hardcore!"

And that was the end of it.

For that night.

But then, three weeks later, we're back for another taping in Queens. Half way through the show, Stevie and Raven climb into the ring and start ragging on me again. So I come out to the ring, and then I slide through the ropes, and I'm standing with my hands on my hips, like, *What's this weenie up to now?*

That's when Richards whips out a sheet of paper and announces that he's suing me for sexual harassment!

The crowd just goes bananas . . . because the fans know about the sexual harassment lawsuit against WCW. It's like they're in on the joke. I don't think I've ever gotten a bigger laugh than when Richards slipped that sheet of paper in my cleavage, like he was serving me, and headed back to the dressing room.

That was my introduction into ECW.

Paul E. put me with Sandman the following week. I didn't mind working with him. He drinks beer 24–7/365 — that's no gimmick, by the way. Lot's of guys didn't want to wrestle him because he was always half-drunk. Plus, sometimes he's got real bad body odor, which is probably related to the drinking too. But he cleans up pretty well. Like I said at the start, his wife Lori Fullington thought we had a fling, but the closest we ever came was once, when we were driving past a cemetery, he turned to me and asked if I'd ever had sex on a grave. He was only joking . . . I think. But just the idea that we *might* have had sex was enough to piss off his wife Lori, which led to her clobbering me with her boot. The main thing about Sandman is that he's got a good heart. After a certain point, especially in a cutthroat business like professional wrestling, you start looking past the money and the fame, and you start going by what's in people's hearts.

One of the first promos I shot with Sandman actually got censored by Madison Square Garden Network, which was carrying ECW at the time. It was a funny bit, a take off on WCW's tag line *WHERE THE BIG BOYS PLAY*. The promo was just me and Sandman, no announcer, no logo in the backdrop. He's chugging beer, and I'm nuzzling up against him, you know, sexing him up. Then I stop, stare into the camera and say, "I've been where the big boys play. And you know the difference between them and us? They spit. . . ."

Then Sandman spits out a mouthful of beer.

"We swallow."

MSG got one look at that promo, and the next morning their public relations manager phoned Paul E. and said, "Unh uh. No way." But Paul E. told me the guy was cracking up.

I had a pretty good time with ECW. We taped on weekends for the most part, and the venues were scattered around the northeast, so the travel time was pretty minimal.

The ECW Arena is in Philadelphia; the place was a converted bingo hall. Vince McMahon used to dis ECW during WWF broadcasts, saying how we were wrestling in a bingo hall. Actually, every time he mentioned us on the air, he did us a favor. But I think he knew that. He kind of regarded ECW as the minor league for the WWF. He would wait for guys to build up their reputations with us, and then he'd sign them away. That's what happened with Mick Foley. He was Cactus Jack with ECW. Then he came to the WWF as Mankind. Then he turned into Dude Love. Then Cactus Jack again. Last I heard, he was going by Mick Foley again, but who can keep track?

I wouldn't cash checks for any of them.

The worst thing about ECW was the ECW Arena. It was a toilet. I mean, we're talking the Le Range Civic Center North. No light in the dressing room. Nowhere to shower. Sticky floors. I mean, it was a dirty, dingy, icky place. I'd have to do my makeup in the car. And I didn't want to change my clothes backstage because whenever the 40 watt bulbs would flicker, you'd catch sight of a roach the size of a terrier.

The wrestlers put up with it though. You'd think there would be all kinds of griping, but these were the hungriest guys I'd ever worked with. They would do *crazy* things to get over. Violent things. I mean, Sabu was doing moonsaults off the top rope and into the crowd; he's like the best, the *craziest* worker I ever saw. Plus, there was not one chair in that arena that wasn't dented in the shape of someone's skull. There's no way to fake that. The chairs being smashed over people's heads, those are real metal folding chairs. I mean, there's a trick to doing it. You aim for the crown of the head with the flat part of the seat; that makes the most noise, and the flat metal's got the most give in it. The Dudley Boys were experts at that. When they used chairs, you could hear the clanging back in the dressing room. But I've seen other guys screw up. Usually, it's the fault of the guy getting hit; he moves at the last second. Young guys especially see the chair coming at them, and their instincts take over. They flinch. Then they get caught with the edge of the seat, not the flat middle, and then it's a mess. But that was the whole idea. It was a blood and guts company.

It was, you know, extreme.

ECW was the organization where wrestlers started getting thrown through tables. Now it's no big deal, just another gimmick; even the major companies have table matches. But the first time I saw Tommy Dreamer go through four tables stacked up, it scared me to death. Because there's no way to control four tables. Going through one table looks bad, but really all the table does is slow down your fall. You just have to watch your head. But two tables is dangerous. You never know what position you're going to be in when you hit the second table. Three tables is crazy. But Tommy was like, "Yeah, yeah, I can do three tables. I can do four."

And he did.

Even the girls in ECW took crazy bumps. I saw Francine get power-bombed through two tables. She's like 110 pounds, and the Pit Bulls launched her from the top rope through two tables outside the ring. I mean, when I saw that, the first thing I thought was: *Whoa, glad that's not me!*

But Francine just shrugged it off. Hey, my hat's off to her. She is the Queen of Extreme. (But she's not the First Lady of Wrestling!) Actually, you wouldn't think it, but she's a real good worker too. When she and Beulah would fight, it looked like they were really kicking the crap out of one another. I mean, you could practically hear the meows. Honestly, I've got nothing bad to say about her.

Beulah, on the other hand, was the biggest bitch. I mean, she wasn't Dark Journey, but she had a *serious* attitude. I tried to put together a calendar, you know, The Women of ECW — that was going to be the title. Francine was as excited as I was. I asked her what months she wanted to pose for, and she said she didn't care. Whatever months weren't taken. Like I said, she was a sweetheart. Kimona Wanalaya too. She picked March and May, so the theme for March was Saint Patrick's Day. She wound up sitting for like two hours in a bathtub full of cold water and green food color, holding up a martini glass until her arm was shaking, smiling for picture after picture. Not a peep out of her. By then, we'd scheduled the rest of the shoots. Miss Alexandra picked her months. But Beulah . . . well, she wasn't into doing it from the start. So I tried to appease her. I saved June for her. That way, she could dress up as a sexy bride. I mean, June was going to be the glamour month! She was set to

Paul E.'s Extreme Girls: kneeling, Kimona; standing (left to right), Francine, me, and Beulah

pose in front of French doors in a white veil and bustier with white stockings and garters. Except instead of a bouquet, she'd be holding a single white rose. Compared with what Kimona went through, it would be a cakewalk. But she whined about it from start to finish, then decided, after we'd already blocked out the camera angles, that she didn't want to do it. She said it wasn't the right image for her.

Hey, the bitch only got into wrestling after she spread her legs in *Cherry Magazine*! She was like Twat of the Month or something. I mean, c'mon, *Cherry Magazine*?

Cherry makes *Hustler* look like freaking *Reader's Digest*!

Yeah, I know. I know. I shouldn't be ragging on Beulah. She's sort of like America's Sweetheart. Or at least Philadelphia's. I guess, by that time, Beulah was planning to get out of the business. She left ECW a couple of months after the calendar thing, so I didn't work with her too much. Anyway, Francine had nothing but nice things to say about her. Beulah's the one who got Francine into wrestling. The two of them were pals from way back. The last I heard, Beulah was going to college. So maybe she'd already decided, even before I came up with the calendar idea, to put the wrestling part of her life behind her. I guess it would be tougher to do that with a photo calendar around to remind you, month after month, of who you used to be. That's the only explanation I can come up with for her freaking attitude.

The one time I did work with Beulah was when she and Kimona were doing their lesbian angle, co-managing Tommy Dreamer. Dreamer was going up against Sandman that night, and the five of us — Dreamer and Sandman, Beulah, Kimona and me — were standing in the ring, waiting for the announcer to introduce us. Suddenly, I hear the crowd going nuts. I glance over my shoulder, and Beulah and Kimona are dancing together, grinding their hips, kissing on the mouth. It was sexy as hell, but at that moment it just pissed me off.

They were getting a bigger pop than I was.

Well, Sandman's got his can of beer, and he's about to bang it open against his forehead, which is his signature move, but I whisper to him, "Pour the beer down my chest."

He looks at me like, *Huh?* He has no idea what I'm talking about because he's got a beer in his hand, and he's got his routine of banging it open against his head and then chugging it down as it foams out of the can, and now I'm telling him to pour it on me.

Then, suddenly, the light bulb goes off — he gets it.

He bangs the can once against his forehead to get it started, and then he bends me backwards by the hair and starts pouring the beer down my neck and breasts. Now, suddenly, no one in the crowd is watching Beulah and Kimona any more.

I mean, no one upstages Missy!

The worst thing that happened to me in ECW was when Lori Fullington broke my elbow — yeah, Sandman's wife, the same wacko bitch who almost knocked my head off with her boot way back in the first chapter. You'd think, after that, she'd have learned her lesson. You know, about being a professional, about keeping her emotions under control. But not Lori. She was jealous, and she didn't want Sandman to work with me anymore, and she finally got to him; Sandman caved in. He told Paul E. he wanted to stop working with me. I mean, I was pissed because we had a good gimmick going. But what the hell? If Sandman was getting heat for working with me, then fine, we'd end it. So he and I started working an angle where we were splitting up, and I was talking trash about him, saying stuff in interviews like, "I don't know how he could be the father of his children because he can't even get it up." I mean, it was just an angle. I knew that. Sandman knew that. Even Lori knew it was just *an angle*. But she's listening to the interview backstage, the start of the blow off, and suddenly, in her mind, it's like I'm telling people she screwed around on Sandman. It's like I'm calling her kids bastards.

I mean, give me a break!

Actually, a couple of weeks later, that's what she did.

We were doing a show in Staten Island; Lori was back at ringside with Raven, and I was with Sandman. It had been a month since she clobbered me with her boot and knocked off my blonde fall. So of course as soon as the four of us — she and Raven, me and Sandman — are in the ring together, Lori and I lunge for one another and start fighting, rolling around, grabbing hair. Then Raven and Sandman pull us apart, but we're still lunging at one another, trying to break free . . . I mean, so far, so good.

By the book.

Now what's supposed to happen next is Lori is supposed to break free and get hold of Sandman's Singapore cane — which he conveniently dropped when he and Raven were pulling us apart. And then she's supposed to run up behind me and crack me across the back with it. So I wriggle free from Sandman, and I'm in position, with my back to her, and I can feel her running up behind me.

I don't know what it was — maybe a kind of sixth sense you develop when you've been in the ring long enough. The moment just felt wrong. I start to peek over my shoulder, and right as I'm peeking, I can hear the *wooosh* of the cane.

The trouble is, it's coming straight at the side of my head. For an instant, I can see it. It's a blur, eye level. Instinctively, I start to duck and put up my right arm.

The can hits me flush in the elbow. Right away, I knew something was really wrong because my entire right arm went limp. I mean, the crazy bitch caned me.

For real.

I managed to roll out under the bottom rope, clutching my elbow. I was so pissed off. I mean, I went crazy. The three of them were still standing in the ring, staring down at me, wondering what to do next, and I was screaming back at them, "Learn how to work, you stupid jaybronees!"

Meanwhile, my knees are getting wobbly. As I started walking up the aisle, back to the dressing room, I remember it was like time was slowing down. I was nauseous from the throbbing in my elbow, and I was listening to the fans on the aisle yelling at me to get back in the ring and fight, and I remember saying to myself, "This is freaking work!" I mean, I'd never walked out on a match before. But it was like in the *Lethal Weapon* movies, where Danny Glover says, "I'm getting too old for this shit." For the first time, right then, as I was staggering up that aisle in Staten Island, I realized wrestling had become a job. And it was a job, suddenly, I didn't want to have.

That's when I knew I had to get out.

Riding to the hospital in the ambulance, I already knew my elbow was broken. I spent a couple of hours sitting in the emergency room, and I kept yelling for a doctor to treat me and let me go — because I knew the matches were just about over, and I wanted to catch a cab back to the arena and kick the shit out of Lori. I mean, I had it planned. I was going to walk right up to her without saying a word and kick the shit out of her. Cast or no cast.

I would've done it too. Except then, just before I was released from the hospital, the doctor gave me a shot of Demerol. So by the time I got back to the arena, I loved everyone.

Anyway, Lori had already left the building.

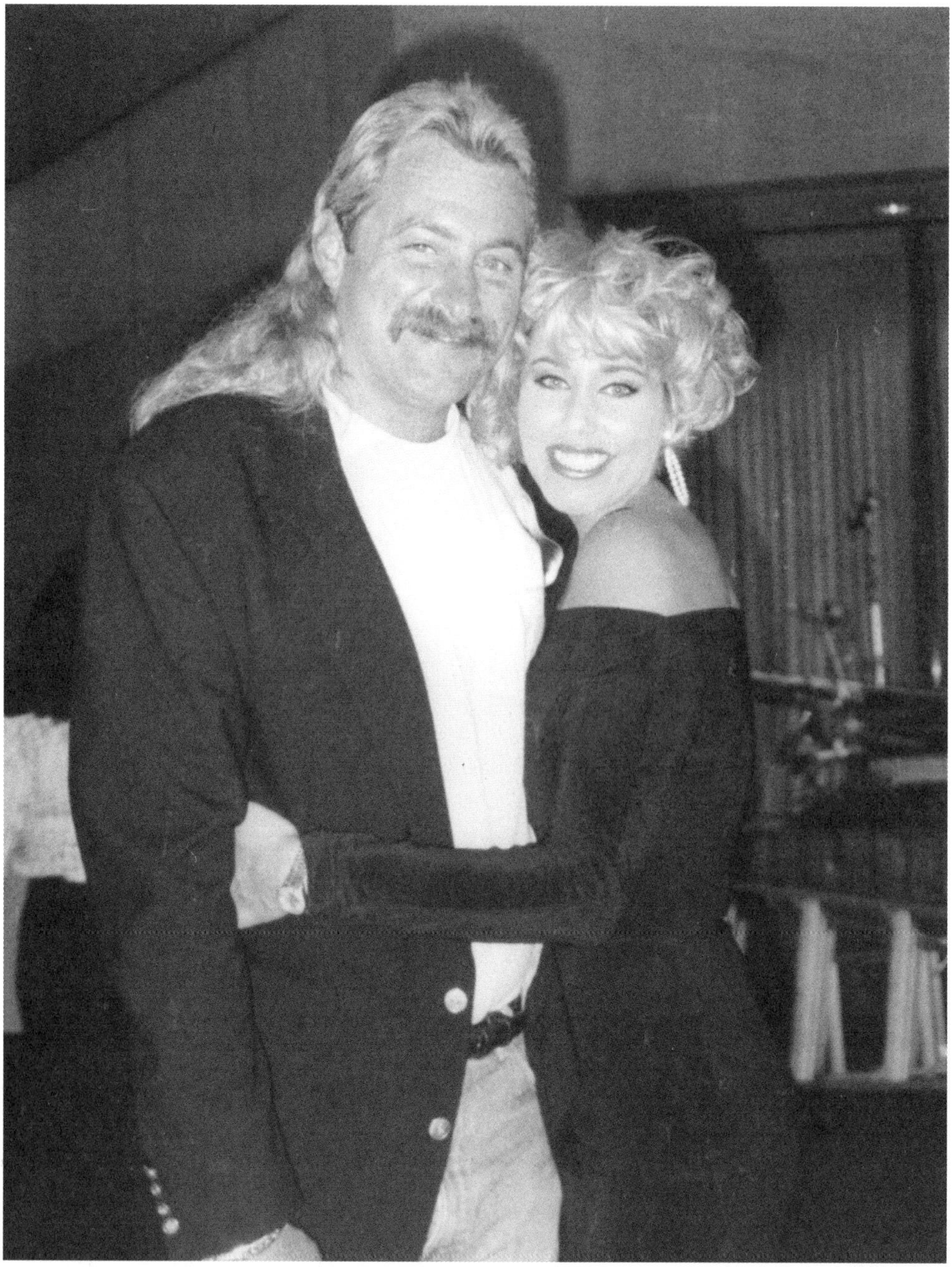

9

Indie-Cent Exposure

Northeast, Independent Organizations

I quit ECW less than a month later. Actually, I asked Paul E. if I could switch to being an announcer. Not a bimbo announcer. I wanted to do it legit. I was even thinking about switching back from *Missy* to *Melissa*. I was tired of being a character, I thought I knew enough about the business to make the transition, to do color commentary as myself. The way Jesse did with the WWF, after he gave up the feather boa.

Paul E. said no way.

That's cinched it. I had to get out. Truthfully, it was real painful. I mean, I *love* Paul E. He saved my sanity for sure, maybe even my life. It was one of the toughest decisions I ever had to make, leaving ECW. What happened with Sandman and Lori was the last straw. But really it was more a matter of knowing when your time's up. Plus, it was just getting too dangerous ringside. Garbage can lids were flying around. Folding chairs were flying around. *People* were flying around. When I started out in the business, I was always worried about what might come out of the crowd. By the end of my time with ECW, I was scared to death of what might come out of the *ring*.

I was almost 35 years old: I needed a change of lifestyle.

Then, out of nowhere, I got a call from Tito Santana. Santana was one of those guys in the business whose path kept crossing with mine. Kind of

With WWF's Road Dog and Kimona

like Road Warrior Hawk — except without the sex.

Santana and Sergeant Slaughter and a couple of suits were putting together a new company, the American Wrestling Federation. They offered me what Paul E. wouldn't — the chance to be a legit announcer. No managing. No catfighting. Just call the matches.

The AWF was set to kickoff its operations with a big press conference at the All Star Café in Times Square. Paul E. got wind of it, and he called me and said he didn't want me at that press conference. I told him I was going, and he told me if I did, he would fire my ass. There was dead silence on the phone.

Then I heard this loud sigh over the phone. It was a real sad sound.

I went to the press conference.

When I got home from the press conference, he fired my ass.

Scott Putski

Right from the start, I knew the AWF was in trouble. The syndication package the suits promised never materialized. The only channels that carried the matches were local stations — and the AWF was paying *them* to televise the cards. No syndication, no money. That's how the business works. No money, not a lot of big name wrestlers. Just the Road Warriors, Animal, and Hawk (yeah, him again), Slaughter and Santana.

All I was doing was announcing.

I taped a few shows for them. But in the end the AWF busted. Naturally, I didn't leave without a romance. I dated Scott Putski — whose father, Ivan, was a famous WWF wrestler in the 1960s and 70s. Scott was kind of a jerk; he was shooting steroids like there was no tomorrow. Plus, the 'roids made him pretty useless in the sack. I mean, the guy looked great standing over the bed, bare-chested, as he pulled off his bathrobe. But then it was like driving a Ferrari with a Volkswagen engine. You rev it up once, and it stalls.

Scott and I stayed together for over a year even after the AWF folded. Tells you what my self-esteem was like around then.

The other fling I had, just a one-nighter, was with Sean Morley — who wrestles in the WWF as Val Venis. For the record, the storyline that he's a former porn star from Las Vegas was pure gimmick. He's from Ontario, Canada. I met Val at an autograph session in New Jersey. He was acting like a big mark, hanging around my table, just staring. He was a big, good-looking guy, and I was on the outs with Putski, so I gave him my number. The next time he was in town, we went out for dinner, then hung out in Times Square, you know, right where the lights are brightest, and afterwards I brought him back to my apartment. We drank a bottle of wine, and I put on the Doors Greatest Hits CD. The song "Light My Fire" had just started when we fell back on the bed. By the time it was over, so was the sex. I mean, it was like the shortest, lamest sex I'd ever had.

Then I was like, "Okay, you got to go. See you around."

Poor guy.

Talk about a guy's gimmick not being him!

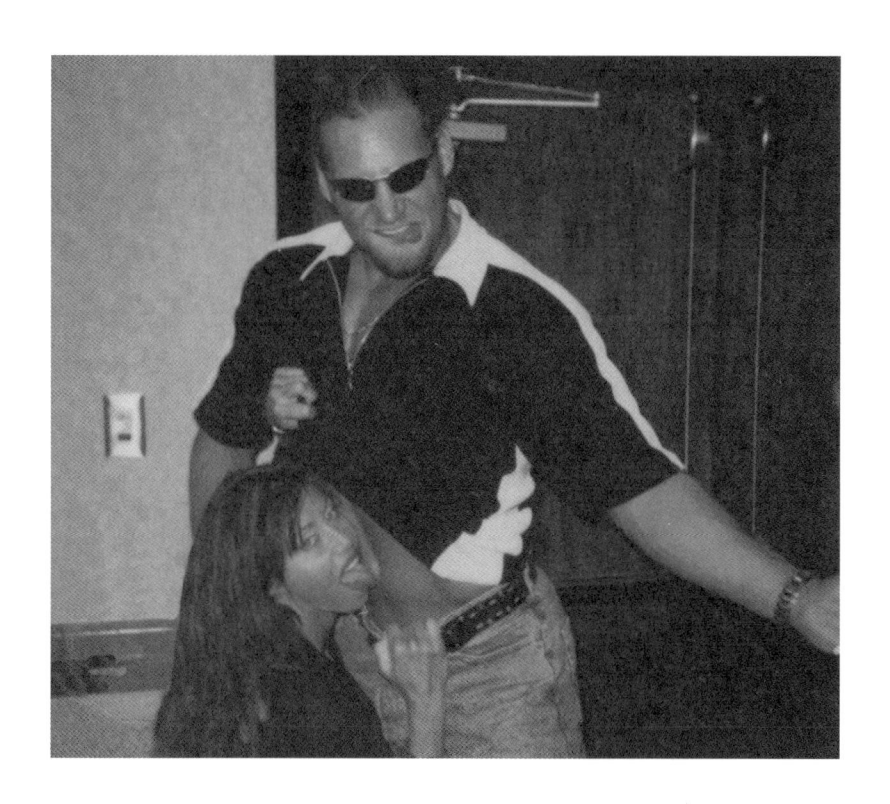

Val Venis

It just goes to show you, wrestling is such a work.

🍸

I guess it had been simmering in the back of my mind for a couple of years to go back to school. So after I left the AWF, I worked indies on the weekends to support myself and took classes during the week to become a medical technician. I earned my certificate in a year, and then I turned to a guy I'd gotten to know real well over the years: my plastic surgeon. He's like a legend in New York City. Tit-doctor to the stars. I strutted into his office with my med tech certificate and asked him for a job.

The next week, I was prepping models and movie stars for boob jobs.

🍸

It was Zena, a girl who worked in the doctor's office, who encouraged me to go back to school for my bachelor's degree. At first I was scared; I didn't know if I could handle college work plus the hours I was putting in at the doctor's office — plus working some indies on the weekends. But Zena told me she'd trade off schedules with me to work around my classes. I still wasn't sure, but she kept after me, and I started checking out college brochures. I finally applied to Marymount Manhattan College. The day I received my acceptance letter was one of the proudest moments of my life.

🍸

That's pretty much where I am now. Still working the Indies. (I even did a sexy 30 second bit with Justin Credible on the last ECW pay-per-view . . . Paul E. never could stay mad at me!) That, plus I'm finishing up my undergraduate degree at Marymount. My major's psychology; my minor is political science. I don't get stares on the street anymore. Sometimes, people almost recognize me; it's like you can read the expressions on their faces: Wait, isn't that . . . nah, it couldn't be her!

I don't want to sound all preachy about it, but education is like maybe the one thing nobody can take away from you. You pay for it. You work for it. Then it's yours. No one can take a percentage off the top. No one can ask for a cut of it in a divorce settlement. It's just yours.

I was sitting in an English class a couple of weeks ago, trying to grasp what the teacher was saying; I remember he was lecturing us about a poem by Edgar Allan Poe called "Annabel Lee." He was talking about metaphors and rhymes, and finally I got frustrated, and I raised my hand and asked, "But what does it mean?"

He just smiled at me and said, "It means whatever you want it to mean. Or it means nothing at all."

I think you could say the same about Missy. She's who I am. She's what I do. I know what she means to me, but she means a million different things to a million different people.

And if you've read this far, she probably means something to you.

Missy . . .

I suppose I'll be trotting her out for a couple of more years at least, on the indie circuit, on weekends. Hey, it pays the bills. But someday soon, I'll be hanging up my pushup bra. The thing is, I've been Missy for over fifteen years now. I think I'd like to give Melissa another shot.

Missy's Top Ten Wrestling Regrets

- Never worked Wrestlemania with the WWF.
- Never got to tell Eddie Gilbert how much I admired him and how much he taught me about the business. (Rest in peace, Hot Stuff.)
- Never kicked Lori Fullington's ass — I mean, for real!
- Never slept with Sweet Stan Lane — a *major* crush!
- Never somersaulted backwards off the top rope.
- Never got a tongue-lashing from Gene Simmons of Kiss. (Yo, Shannon — you go, girl!)
- Never gave Sunshine enough credit for showing me how to catfight.
- Never lewinskied Jesse Ventura. (Hey, who knew?)
- Never studied psychology while I was still active in the business.
- Never got that Missy Doll. (Bastards!)